# Give Him ~~Back~~ His Balls

For Happy Relationships

To dear Danhee and Bob,

So wonderful to know you,

Much Love,

Brigitte

# Give Him Back His Balls

## For Happy Relationships

Brigitte Sumner

Published by MVP 2007

My Voice Publishing
Unit 1 16 Maple Road
EASTBOURNE
BN23 6NY
United Kingdom

www.myvoicepublishing.com

Published by MVP 2007-01-21

Cover design: Studio Jan De Boer
Design: Zuidzeven, Asten, The Netherlands
Cover photograph: Tommy Candler
ISBN 978-0-9554692-0-6

# Contents

# Introduction

Why do men need their balls back? Why have women ended up with the balls in relationships? Why do so many high powered, single women seem unable to get into a relationship? Is it possible to revamp a desperate and soulless relationship? Over the many years of coaching of groups and individuals I have applied and tested the suggestions in this book.

I have been happily and unhappily married to my husband Rex for the past 18 years. When we started dating we were completely smitten with each other. We could not live, breathe, eat or do anything without one another. In fact, for the first year that we were together, we did not spend a single day apart. Many people felt our relationship was too close. For us, we just could not imagine a day without the other. We knew from a very early stage in our relationship that we wanted to spend the rest of our lives together. Both of us were in our late twenties and had had many other partners before. Both of us knew that this was different. This was in the mid eighties. We met in Indonesia in an international social setting and moved to the UK in the late eighties, where both our sons were born. During the whole of the nineties things were not going well in our relationship. The symptoms were very much a loss of passion and love. We were living like brother and sister or best friends at the best of times. I was just starting on a journey of personal development and felt a desperate need for Rex to change. He felt he was fine as he was, thank you very much. I felt that I had to do everything. I felt that he was behaving like one of the children. I longed for the intimacy and passion we had had earlier in our relationship before the dissatisfaction crept in. With the way we had both started to behave over the years, this was impossible. It is not that we had big rows (although occasionally we did). It is not that we had lost sexual interest in each other. It is not that we were interested in other men and women. It was simply not the way it used to be. It took the best part of a decade to resolve our issues, during which time I was grieving for what I felt I had lost. I felt that maybe a relationship just evolved to be like that once you were together for a few years; after all I had evidence of what most people's relationships looked like all around me. As I am not one to easily give up, I kept seeking to find our love, our passion and that special love we once had. And I found all of it and more. I learned how to live in my feminine energy in my intimate relationship. I learned how to give my husband back his balls.

Now Rex and I have a solid and soul-mate relationship that is not the same as when we started but it in many ways is even better, very passionate, warm, playful, trusting and based on mutual honesty. We have a lot of fun together, we have more of the dialogue that we used to have, and there is a connection that wasn't there before. We have come together again on a common shared vision which had been lost and disguised for years. We are proud to be together, our (now teenage) sons sometimes shake their heads when they witness our love, our silly playfulness and our passion. It is the healthiest and best relationship education they could ever receive.

When I tell my own story, there is invariably a recognition, an 'aha' moment where many people realise that this is exactly what has gradually happened in their own relationship. I hear many men and women say that they too are in the situation where they feel they have lost something and yet can't put their finger on what it is or where to find it. The reason we enter a long term intimate relationship is that we have the expectation of so much pleasure. Yet, a lot of relationships are a source of so much pain. I have noticed specifically in my coaching practice that a lot of women and men go through the pain of these symptoms of loss. I have helped and worked with a lot of individuals and groups to alleviate the pain and bring back the total pleasure and fulfillment that an intimate relationship can give. I feel that it is now time that more people get to know that there is a way to get out of the relationship impasse, a way which is easy, fun, do-able and certainly faster than the decade it took us.

As women have moved forward so much over the last fifty years by becoming equal career wise, we've also taken that into the area of our intimate relationships. This is one area where this type of 'equality' doesn't work because in order for there to be passion there needs to be polarity.

The things you will learn in this book are a progression, not something that reverts back. This is a step forward from where we are now and many steps forward from where we were before the onset of the women's liberation. This book will enable you to re-ignite the passion in your own relationship, whilst keeping all the gains that we have had from womens' movements.

Let me first share a little about myself. I am half Dutch and half Chinese, born in Amsterdam. At the age of twenty seven I took a trip to Beijing, China to visit my paternal grandmother who I had seen last when I was just six months old. While there I became intrigued by Chinese medicine, philosophies and traditions. The Yin and the Yang are infinitely important polar opposites. One does not exist without the other. I have a thriving Feng Shui and coaching business. I have trained and worked with Anthony Robbins, Deepak Chopra, John Gray, Jay Abraham, Brandon Bays, Judy May Murphy, Wayne Dyer and various NLP masters and investment and health experts.

Who is this book for? This book is for women who are in a relationship and want to improve it, for women who have been in a relationship and don't want to make the same mistakes again, for women who are raising boys to be men and girls to be happy women and for any woman who needs to interact with any man at any stage in her life. It can be read by men who want insight into the dynamic of relationships and are seriously committed to improving their relationship. It's for men who want to understand women, be they their lovers, mothers, daughters, or any other woman they interact with in their lives. So, if you are a human being and you live on this planet (or any other) then you can benefit from reading this book.

Perhaps your relationship is at breaking point, or perhaps it is just not exciting you or making you feel good in the way it did in the past. Wherever you are at in your relationship, this book will guide you to a place where you feel filled up and satisfied with the way you and your partner live, love, interact and communicate together again.

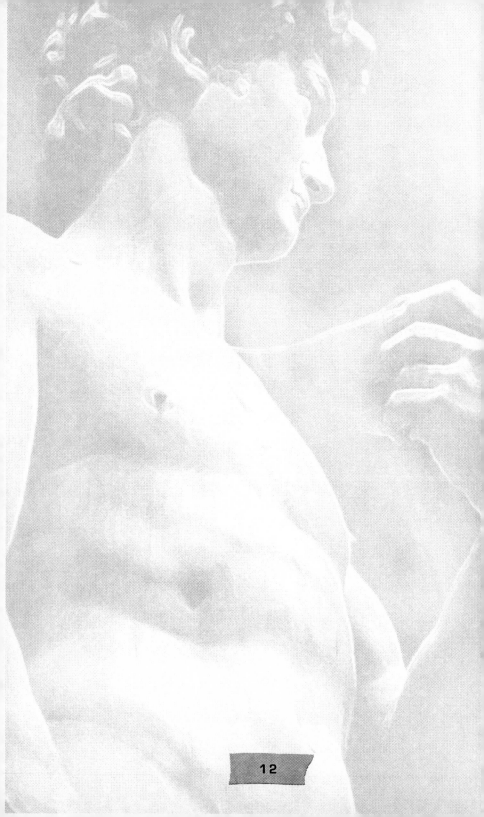

12

# Chapter One
# Why Balls?

Balls are a symbol of masculinity. All men have them and there are a lot of sayings about balls such as 'He's got no balls', 'you know whose got the balls in this relationship', 'handing him his balls on a plate', 'it takes balls to say that', 'you need to get your balls back' etc. Give Him Back His Balls is meant in jest and at the same time very seriously. It is time to step in and look at what we can do to re ignite the lost passion in our relationships. It is time as women to stop being masculine in our intimate relationship as it does not work! It is time to 'give him back his balls'. You will find that if you do, your relationship with the man in your life (be it your husband, boy-friend, brother, father, son, boss or employee) will improve hugely.

Balls are a man's Achilles heel. Even small amounts of pressure or friction or impact can hurt a lot and disable a man for a long time. Physically it is a 'weak' area and men don't like to be seen as weak as they tend to consider that as a feminine trait. If a man is castrated then a lot of men (and women) don't consider him to be a man anymore. Even a man who contemplates 'the snip' because he doesn't want any more children, will consider it carefully because cutting off the connection to the balls can give the man the false impression that his identity of a man has been weakened.

Physiologically your man has balls. Does he have them mentally?

What I mean by this is 'Does he play the masculine role in the relationship?'

In order to answer this question we need to know what the masculine and feminine roles are and what they have been historically.

Historically, men were supposed to provide food, money, protection and shelter for the woman in their life. Women were expected to provide nurturing, food preparation, child rearing and housekeeping. Let's illustrate this with a little story.

Once upon a time there was a medieval man called Angus. He lived in a picturesque little village amidst glowing meadows and forests. There was a gentle stream flowing by the cosy hamlet. While in his late teens he fell in love with a beautiful fair-haired maiden called Isobel. Isobel was the talk of the little village they lived in. She was desired by all the young men, as she was not only beautiful to look at but witty and smart at the same time, without being defiant. She would be at the village dances and have flowers in her hair which was golden and dropped down to her tiny waist. Angus was taller than most of the lads in his village with handsome features and a good hunting eye. He was whispered about by most of the young ladies in the village for his agile body, his witty mind and his tireless energy when it came to hunting, building and making weaponry. Angus was regarded a good 'catch' and so was Isobel. After they had spent some months stealing private moments going for walks around the woods and swimming in the stream, the pair became inseparable and Angus decided he wanted to marry Isobel. He went to her father to ask for her hand (the women were not consulted). Between the men it was decided how big the dowry was to be. In this case, Isobel's father hands over 15 sheep, a brass cooking pot, 2 sleeping mats, 20 cow hides, an ox and a horse. During their marriage Angus is very clear on his tasks and brings in the food. Once a week he returns from hunting with his friends and places in the cooking pot a brace of hare, or a pheasant and occasionally a boar or deer. As one of the footmen for the local squire he brings home coins for buying flour to make bread, clothing and shoes. They live in the house which he built with his bare hands and most of the furniture is made by him during the long winter evenings. He protects his family physically from invading marauders by fighting them off with the sword which he wears in his belt at all times. Only at night does he take the sword off and place it beside his bed, sleeping on the door-side in order to defend his family.

Isobel's task is also much defined and she knows from the onset that she has to do the cooking, washing, child bearing and rearing, the sewing and mending and other household chores. She probably also knows that when he wants sex she has to provide that service too.

One day Angus goes hunting and is pursued by a hoard of wild boar. He's been drinking ale in the inn so his footing is slightly unstable, it is snowing and he slips and is mauled to death by the savage pigs. When Isobel hears the tragic news she is beside herself with grief and desperation for her own future and that of her children. She does not have the skill, nor the inclination, to be able to provide all that her man has done up until his death. She does not know how to hunt and neither does she have the will to learn to hunt, nor is it socially accepted that she would do so as a woman. She can't go out and work in Angus's old position to provide her with money. She is fearful for the welfare and lives of herself and her three small children and feels totally defenseless against brigands and fiends. Although she still cooks, mends and raises the children, there is no income and she cannot function on her own.

Well..., we really miss Angus so let's revive him. Angus is alive and well once more. Let us now look at the opposite scenario. Isobel has a very tough time during the birth and labour of their third child, a big and heavy eight pound baby boy in breach position. Even though the local women did everything to try to save Isobel, she became increasingly weak during the thirty hour ordeal. The baby was saved but unfortunately Isobel died. Now Angus is on his own with three children, all under five years old and with no clue how to take care of them. During his grieving period, the little bairns scream and cry for food and drink. Angus is desperate but doesn't know what to do. The house gets run down, the family's clothes get shabby, the vegetable patch does not get tended to, the crop gets eaten by the hungry goat that does not get fed and the chickens' escape which means that the family has no more eggs. He still provides meat and coin and sword defense but without the feminine input the family cannot survive.

Things didn't really change much until the 1970s in the western world.

During this time men could still do what they did before (namely provide food, money and defense) but gradually, over time, it became socially acceptable for them to be nurturing of the family and themselves. They began to cook, garden, clean and do more household chores. Women could still do what they did before (namely nurture and tend) but it also became socially acceptable for them to work outside the house and defend themselves physically.

Long ago, actually not that long ago, (the 1970s in fact) there lived a couple named Richard and Felicity. Richard is an energetic and talented young man in his early twenties and he has fallen in love with Felicity. Felicity is not only the 'belle of the ball' but she is also pretty and has a head for numbers. They went to the same school and have been going out together for a while. They moved in together when they both went to university. They shopped together, cooked together and repaired their Deux Chevaux together whenever it broke down, which was fairly often. They would enjoy spending time together and would be sharing all their tasks equally.

Whenever Felicity went to Paris with a couple of girl-friends, Richard did his own laundry, cooked chili con carne and other experimental dishes. When Richard went to visit his elderly parents who lived up North, Felicity went out with her friends to the local pub for a couple of beers after her evening job. When the car broke down it was no bother for her to do the required minor repairs. After student life they bought a small house in a suburb together and soon after Felicity became pregnant. Both of them read pregnancy and baby books and they went to the ante-natal classes together. When the baby was born, Richard was present and even changed the newborn's first nappy whilst Mum was recovering. They had two more children and shared the child rearing and both had full time jobs.

One day Richard announces that he needs to search for his soul to find out who he really is. While he's off in India with an enlightened guru for three months, Felicity and the three children cope very well. Felicity is able to both provide food and money and nurture and tend to herself and the children.

On Richard's return the lifestyle of the family hasn't really changed. After this long break Richard is able to slide back into the family unit as if nothing has happened. A year later Felicity is invited by a Canadian university to do a three month research project. The children and Richard see her off at the airport and resume their lives undisturbed with Richard cooking healthy and nutritious meals, providing cuddles, overseeing homework, while still doing his day job. When Felicity returns the couple discuss the experience and find that it has been enriching for all.

Even though they have missed each other, on seeing the other person again there are no great sparks flying. Felicity realises that they never really have had a passionate relationship. Or that from the onset of the relationship, the passion soon went. We see in this couple that although they are able to function very well without the other, there is more camaraderie and friendship than an intimate relationship with polarity and passion.

The reason this couple have had no passion in their relationship is because both of them operate from a neutral sexual energy, rather than a definite masculine or feminine energy.

Without meaning to stereotype, masculine energy is defined by a tendency to be outgoing, to achieve, to be driven, ambitious, obsessed, logical, determined, motivated, focused, single-minded and linear. A man can only focus on one thing at a time. He cannot drive and listen to you talking at the same time. If you want to read some more about that, I suggest you read the hilarious and informative book 'Why men don't listen and women can't read maps' (see booklist). Your man is so focused on his target and where he wants to go that he can tune out background noises and not be distracted by anything. In ancient times when Angus went hunting this was particularly beneficial as he could laser-focus on the deer in front of him and not on whatever was happening in his peripheral vision. Men are solution oriented. Give them a problem and they will solve it. In fact, they look for challenges and love them so much that they sometimes see them when they are not even there. They are competitive and want to win, which is evident in the way they gather status, material wealth and go about sports and other leisure pursuits. They are compatible with Yang, fire, energy, sun, creation, heat, light, Heaven and dominance.

Feminine energy is receiving, flowing, nurturing, lateral, emotional, all-seeing, caring, creating, gentle, compassionate and tidal. Women's moods can quickly swing from one extreme to another. Women are able to multitask, they can simultaneously chop vegetables, whilst overseeing homework and talk to a child's teacher on the telephone. A woman finds it hard to stay focused exclusively and not be distracted by what is going on around her. This allows her to be aware of more than one thing. The benefit of this to Isobel was that she was able to tend to her children whilst feeding the chickens and talking to her visiting sister at the same time. Women are connection orientated, give them a problem and they'll talk about it. They are more about the team and giving everybody a fair chance, which is evident in the way they conduct their lives and interact with the world. They are compatible with Yin, the moon, completion, cold, darkness and material forms.

Masculine and feminine energies complement and attract each other like opposite poles on a magnet. We all have masculine and feminine energies and are all able to display parts of both. Most men have stronger masculine energy and most women have stronger feminine energy. The stronger the masculine energy the stronger feminine energy this will attract. A weaker masculine energy attracts a weaker feminine energy. In our example of Isobel and Angus, our medieval couple, it was evident that each had strong masculine or feminine energy. In our example of Richard and Felicity, our seventies couple, it showed that each had a weaker masculine and feminine energy as they both took on tasks that needed both energies. Richard was a go-getter when he was in his career and was nurturing when he was at home. His trip to India to find himself displayed largely feminine energy. Felicity's energies were also displaying both an achiever's outlook which represents a masculine energy and was compassionate when with her family, which represents the feminine energy.

Women and men no longer depend on each other the way Isobel and Angus did, so when men and women decide to live together this is more out of choice than necessity. What this has given society is a huge amount of feminine high-powered careers. It has also led to the ability for women to choose to be in a relationship or not. For the first time in history women have been able to get out of abusive relationships without massive implications. Women have been able to work outside the home, study and in theory reach as high a level in anything as men. They are able to excel at sports, in academics, politics, sciences, labour, entertainment, adventure, creativity, general leadership and even lately in spiritual leadership. Men have felt the pressure to exclusively provide was taken off them as women would provide some, half, or most of the household income.

This meant that men don't have to work all hours. They have more time to get to know their children and be more involved in their upbringing. They are able to find more time for connection to themselves, friends and family and explore their emotional side.

The drawbacks to men living in both masculine and feminine energies and women living in both masculine and feminine energies are becoming evident in relationships now. The biggest problem is that because there is lack of polarity, there is lack of passion. Because there is lack of passion, both parties feel that they are less happy and fulfilled. Because they are less happy and less fulfilled, all types of challenges start to occur. It can be that one or both parties feel misunderstood, so they may look elsewhere for understanding and start an affair. It can be that one or both parties feel frustrated, so they may start to indulge in less healthy habits such as overeating, drinking, or smoking. It may be that one or both parties feel unhappy, so they may get depressed. All of the above can result in physical manifestation of what the heart is suffering from.

What we see in modern relationships is that there is so much 'equality' that the women are not feminine and the men are not masculine enough to attract each other. In many Western European countries we see men and women who look the same with the same short haircut, dress the same with shorts and t-shirts, walk the same and use the same language. The dynamics you notice between people like that, is that they are very good friends but there is no romance or no sexual difference as you see in places like Southern European and South American countries, where the men are dressed in very masculine clothes and the women in very feminine clothes. In those cultures, men tend to have short hair and women tend to have long hair. This is a symbol of how they traditionally manifest their natural energies. By no means does it imply that the hair style or clothing is the be-all and end-all when it comes to being masculine or feminine. The 'feminine mask' of the power dressed executive on stiletto heels can cover a masculine core. When you see a Latin couple together you can sense the sexual attraction between them. Women seem to be conscious of their body and proud of it, regardless of shape and age. I have seen women in their late sixties who in our culture would be called overweight, dancing seductively and sensuously in tight and colourful spandex in the town square in Puerto Rico during the local carnival, something you wouldn't see much in the western world.

Often, when the woman takes on a high proportion of the masculine energy in a relationship, we can say that she is wearing the balls.

In the following examples you will meet four couples where in each situation the man is no longer wearing the balls.

Jenny and Paul have been married for twenty years, seemingly happy to the outside world. They have no children and spend their time socialising a lot. They also play tennis together. Paul works as a senior partner in a legal firm and Jenny has her own business in the health arena. Paul has found lately that Jenny seems to nag him more and more about jobs that he needs to do around the house. Paul likes to please Jenny but feels that lately she is taking advantage of his good nature. He has not communicated this with her but is waiting for a change of course. She has made all the decisions as to what has to happen in the house without even consulting him and he feels that he is just being used as a handyman.

**She is wearing the balls.**

Ahmed and Sonita have been going out together for three years. Sonita is a bookkeeper at a large department store and Ahmed is a sales rep. Because Sonita is a bookkeeper it seemed logical early on in their relationship that she would look after their joint financial affairs. Any time they go on holiday or outings together it is Sonita who handles the money and calculates and budgets their spending. Their relationship started out being very romantic but more and more Sonita has the feeling that although having control is nice on one level, she somehow doesn't feel good about it. Ahmed seems to be alright with her handling all their money and this complacency seeps into other areas of their relationship.

**She is wearing the balls.**

Phoebe and Hector have lived together for six years. They have a daughter, Beate, and Hector's elderly mother lives with them. Phoebe is a very caring and compassionate person. Hector works as an insurance agent and Phoebe is at home with their young child. Phoebe spends her time running around the house looking after and waiting-on her mother-in-law and the baby. When Hector comes home after a long day at work, Phoebe stays in the same mode and mothers him too. She reminds him to wear a clean vest every day, feeds him his vitamin supplements and tells him to take an umbrella when it rains. When they are at a party she will nudge him gently and say 'enough, dear', when in her mind he has had enough alcohol to drink. Hector feels increasingly dissatisfied and less sexually attracted to his partner.

**She is wearing the balls.**

Judy and Gabriel have been blissfully married for four years and have twins. They have been submerged in sleepless nights and overwhelmed by the work that two little people have brought into their relatively structured lives. Both of them have a career, Judy is a successful illustrator of children's books and Gabriel is an estate agent. They work odd hours and even though they have a nanny, Judy feels that she has had to take responsibility for everything. She makes the decisions on the twins upbringing, hires and fires household staff, decides and arranges the couple's social arrangements, buys all their clothes, arranges their holidays and chooses their cars. All Gabriel does is show up. One morning Judy wakes up crying. Gabriel asks what the matter is and she tells him that it feels like she is doing everything on her own, that she has no support and that he is just like a well-kept lodger. She feels sexually unattractive as she is always exhausted and can't even switch off her brain in bed. Gabriel hasn't noticed a thing and has just been happy that everything is working like a well-oiled machine. It comes as a complete revelation to him.

**She is wearing the balls.**

Isn't it logical that Jenny repeatedly asks for the jobs around the house to be done?

Doesn't it make sense that Sonita handles the money because she is the book keeper?

Why shouldn't Phoebe remind Hector of things that he would otherwise forget?

If Judy is good at organising and arranging why wouldn't she manage and oversee their lives?

Yes, it may be logical. Absolutely it might make sense. Why not indeed? You are totally right.

**BUT IT DOESN'T WORK!**

In all the above examples the woman is wearing the balls.

So, picture all these couples in twenty years time.

During the following decade Paul retreated inside himself. He now spends more and more time in his shed doing his DIY projects. They hardly ever play tennis together as Paul has found excuses to avoid this previously pleasant pass time more and more. As he feels that Jenny is still nagging him and doesn't understand him, he prefers to be on his own or spend time with friends. The annual holiday is spent together but feels awkward and they are both relieved when they get back home and can lead their separate lives again. Jenny is increasingly involved in the WI and her flower arranging classes. She does not understand where things went wrong but blames it on the fact that all relationships dilute with time.

Twenty three years after they first met Sonita and Ahmed are the parents of two boys, one who is at university and one who is doing his GCSEs. Sonita is still managing the family finances and is doing bookkeeping for other families. Ahmed is now a sales manager for the area. Because their mother is so strong with the finances the boys haven't really learned how to deal with money either. Both of them still go to Mum for pocket money and the eldest one, who is at university, burns through money like a bushfire. Neither of them has any sense of the worth of money nor any sense of financial responsibility. The relationship between Ahmed and Sonita is amicable. They go out to family functions and on family holidays but they never go on dates together as neither of them feels compelled to do so and Sonita feels that she is taking him out (because she pays) and Ahmed has long lost the feeling that he can do anything special for his wife because she has control of the money.

In Hector and Phoebe's situation, things went from bad to worse. During the first decade after we met them, Hector's Mum died and Phoebe had more time to mother Hector more intensely. She became increasingly concerned about whether he was wearing a coat or not when it was cold and would even ring him up at work to ask whether she should bring him in a scarf. It got even worse after their daughter went to boarding school. Phoebe put all her mothering attentions onto poor Hector. She made him healthy salads every day to take to the office so that he would not go to the pub, she monitored his drink by marking the whisky bottle with a marker and she put out his clothes for him the night before. She would even monitor his TV watching and switch off the TV at eleven sharp regardless of what he was watching under the pretence that he needed his eight hours sleep. Hector felt controlled and rebelled against this by drinking outside the house and starting an affair with his secretary. When Phoebe found this out she filed for divorce. They have been divorced for the past six years.

Judy and Gabriel moved to Florida when Gabriel was able to retire. Judy has made their home really glamourous and constantly changes the décor. Gabriel has bought a lot of real estate in Florida and Judy spends her time decorating and designing the interiors for all of them when they rent them out. Gabriel spends his time in his office at home doing his internet trading and is at the beck and call of his charismatic wife. Whenever they go out do dinner parties she is the life and soul of the party who flirts and chats with everyone whilst he is the quiet wallflower. The twins are both at Harvard and whist they have a lot of fun with their gregarious Mum, they make fun of their Dad who they don't respect and feel contempt for because they notice the role reversal that has crept into their parent's relationship. They are growing up without a true understanding of what their role, as males in a relationship will be. They act irresponsibly with drink and experiment with drugs, whilst they have a lot of one night stands, never really spending any in depth time with any female. Deep down Judy feels sad at the loss of what once was but she keeps herself so busy with all her social and other engagements that she prefers to block out the emotion. Gabriel feels content with their material wealth. He admires his wife and believes that a passionate relationship is something for teenagers and the fact that they don't have sex anymore is a natural progression in a relationship.

So where are you in your relationship? Who is wearing the balls in your relationship? Does it resemble any of the above scenarios? Maybe it's a mixture of several of them?

Where will you be in twenty years time if you keep going on in the same way?

## Chapter Two

# Why we should give him back his balls

As women we have ended up with the balls in our relationships. We feel we have to juggle everything, we feel we have to organise the family, the holiday, the home, and the schedules for the family. We feel that we have to phone the dentist, make the appointment and cart the family member there. We feel that we have to design the house, arrange for the building of it, furnish it, keep it clean and repaired and functioning. We feel that we have to look for the holiday, book it, sort out the house sitting arrangements and pack for the whole family. We may have a career besides our household and children and be the boss, the manager, the organiser and may have to keep a whole business and office functioning and keep healthy and fit. Besides that we may have several hobbies or other commitments that take our time. It is simply wonderful that we do all the above. And yes, I am one of those new age women who can do it all, who can have it all and I thrive on it. The only place this behaviour is not working is in my relationship. I achieve, I am focused, I drive, I pursue as much as the next man. When I do this in my relationship with Rex, it does not work. From our previous chapter we have seen that if we women wear the balls in our relationship, it doesn't work. We get too much into our masculine energy and neither person feels good. When we have the balls and predominantly operate from a masculine energy source (being driven, solution oriented, having big and linear vision, able to focus on one subject only, etc) in our relationship we can get really tired, controlling, and pedantic which is not attractive to a man. What that does is cause him to react to us as if we were another man. He will argue, he will compete, take us for granted, negate our feelings, be irritated and constantly be on guard as he would be with another man. He will not want to go out with us and be romantic and the last thing on his mind is to have passionate sex with us!

On the other hand, when we are in our feminine energy (nurturing caring, gentle, multi-tasking, flowing, creating, team-oriented etc) in our relationship, we stay fresh, going with the flow, living in the moment, dealing with challenges as they come up, staying happy and content. This is attractive to a man. His natural reaction is to give love and attention to us when we are in this state. A man's main purpose for being in a relationship is to make his woman happy. When he sees that he succeeds at this he feels he has accomplished his outcome which makes a man feel proud and confident. When he feels proud and confident he is able to go out into the world and deal with whatever comes his way in business, social situations and family situations.

**Is there any time that women need balls?**

There are some times that it is useful to keep some balls at hand. I always get amused when the boss of a company I do contract work for complains that the women executives are not feminine enough. What he probably means is that they have balls in the work place, and keep wearing them in their personal life. In certain instances it is useful to have balls. Nicola Horlick would not have progressed to where she is now if she did not have balls in her career. Margaret Thatcher needed to have the balls of the nation (in the handbag?) when in charge of Britain. There are situations where having balls is appropriate. When your house is on fire, it pays to keep your head cool and get out the nearest door, saving your nearest and dearest in the process. When your child is about to choke on a boiled sweet, you want to give him a good thump between the shoulder blades in order for him to spit the culprit out. When you have just managed to 'park' your car in the canal, it is helpful to have the clarity of thought and be able to save yourself and children by opening the sunroof or bashing your side window with the fire extinguisher. Have balls for the occasions that you need them.

How did we end up with these balls in the first place? In a situation where a man was not paying attention or not taking action where it was required, you possibly took the lead and made a decision for both of you. Here are some possible examples you may relate to.

• You were driving along a country road and he did not know the way. Rather than let him find out from the map or even by trial and error, you got out at the nearest shop and asked for directions. What that does is take your man's masculine power away. When this is just an isolated incident and not part of a habit this will just be a glitch that will be forgotten after a while. If, on the other hand, this is the start of a habit it will be an experience that time and time again will remind him of his failure to carry out his masculine duties. A better way of dealing with a situation like this is to zip your mouth shut, sit on your hands and look out of the window whilst you tell him that you are confident that he will get you there. This way you leave him with his balls and remind him of his masculine energy which loves and solves problems. Once he works out where to go he feels great and proud that he has got you there. 'So what' if you are now an hour behind schedule? At least you have given him the great gift of feeling that he sorted it out for both of you.

- You were already making sandwiches for the children and so you made a lunch for him without consulting him on the matter. How does this make him feel? He might be pleasantly surprised and think you are thoughtful but on the other hand if this is the beginning of ongoing mothering behaviour he will feel controlled by you. Instead of taking the initiative to make his sandwiches, either ask him if he would like it, or wait until he asks you. This way you leave him with his balls and masculine power to decide for himself what he eats for lunch.

- You were at a party where you were talking to people and when they asked your man a question, you answered for him. 'Brad, what line of work are you in?'

You answer: 'He's an accountant with Parsons and Parsons on the Green.' If this happens occasionally because he is just not listening or has taken a huge bite of a vol-au-vent, this is absolutely fine. If this is a pattern that recurs regularly, you undermine his power. You want to be mindful not to speak for your man (or anyone else) on a regular basis even when they are occupied with something else. The person who asks the question will be courteous enough to repeat the question or attract your man's attention in another way. Your man will feel that you've left his personal power intact and trusted him to speak for himself in his own time.

• You have always been used to carrying your own luggage and being self-sufficient. Now you meet a man and he offers to carry your bags for you. You say, 'Thank you, I can manage,' and carry them yourself. The message that this gives to him is that he has been rejected and is not needed and is unable to make you happy in this situation. We know that you, like most women, are perfectly capable of carrying any amount of luggage, open any doors, change any tyre at any time, pull out any chair and put on your own coat. However, performing these small tasks for you makes your man feel he has done something to make you happy and that is what he is about. He feels useful, appreciated, and masculine.

**So how did I end up with the balls in my own relationship?**

When my husband Rex and I met in Indonesia, he was the person who could speak the language fluently and knew Jakarta, which was where we lived. He would take me out to fun places such as Seafood 99, a tent by the side of the road where you could get the best seafood in town, if you could stomach the shabby surrounds, and to Pelabuhan Ratu, the best beach on our side of the island of Java, with gorgeous white sand that would stretch for miles and miles and not a human in sight apart from the odd fisherman, seafood and coconuts galore.

After a year we moved to England where I soon became pregnant with our eldest son Jeremy. I had lost my confidence during a spell of typhoid and Rex thought that if he let me make more decisions and take charge of our family life, I would regain my confidence. So I arranged the buying of our house in England, the mortgage, the move and from then on, pretty soon I seemed to be arranging everything from family holidays to buying everyone's clothes. I would also handle the family finances.

A typical conversation between Rex and I would go like this:

**Brigitte:** I think we need to sell the house,

Rex: Why?

**Brigitte:** So that we can reduce our overheads and move closer to Jeremy's school.

Rex: Ok, if that's what you would like.

**Brigitte:** I've already seen some places and this place in Stone Cross really appeals. It has four bedrooms, three reception rooms, an office for me to conduct my coaching business and a driveway for the cars. The rent is very reasonable.

Rex: That sounds nice.

**Brigitte:** It's also only ten minutes from the school, and I think that's where we should send Lionel too. I'll contact them to arrange a viewing on Saturday.

**I was wearing the balls!**

At this time I felt completely in charge of everything and whilst it was sort of a good feeling to have all this control and certainty, it felt very bad in other ways. I was feeling increasingly drained, exhausted, sad, unappreciated, overwhelmed and unhappy but I would quickly mask those feelings with masculine feelings of anger, irritation, impatience and dismissive-ness. I was constantly tired, felt unwomanly and unloved. Rex felt totally un-attracted to me, useless, lazy, unable to make decisions (because any he made would be instantly disapproved of by me anyway) and resentful. He would criticise me in company as it seems that this was the only way he could get back at me for emasculating him.

I realised that I was so unhappy and we were not the couple we had been in the beginning. I felt the relationship had fallen apart and it was time for both of us to break up and move on. I did not think that the damage to the relationship could be repaired and saw no other solution than to separate. One afternoon in early spring I was weeding the garden and couldn't see the flowers through my tears. I remembered all the good times we'd had and all the precious memories we had built up over the years. I felt that this was too beautiful to just give up on. I remembered in my heart that Rex and Brigitte were soul mates and were meant to be together.

**Something needed to change.**

Over the years I came to realise that I had got into the masculine habit of directing, controlling and leading and this was not congruent with my feminine nature. I came to the conclusion that this was the reason why I was so exhausted. I decided to give him back his balls.

This was a painful process as I had become very attached to them. Up to now everything would happen exactly the way I wanted it to happen, on my terms and to my specifications. By this time, Rex was feeling quite comfortable without them as it gave him the opportunity to focus on his work only.

**So, what did I do?**

I changed my choice of words from saying 'This is what we are going to do' instead saying 'I would love to do this, what do you think?' Now I even say 'I would love to have this' and leave it open to give him the opportunity to step up and make it happen of his own accord.

When we were going out for an evening I began to let him surprise me with his choice of restaurants and movies. Even though they would not have been my first choice I knew it was important for him to flex his masculine muscles and I felt good being taken care of.

It sounds as if it was very easy, simple and fast. In a way it was but it took a lot of trial and error before I got it right. And I still don't get it right all the time. The thing is that you do not need to be perfect at it to notice huge changes and differences. It is so rewarding once you start to 'give him back his balls!'

What would have happened if the women from the examples in the previous chapter had decided to give their men back their balls?

If Jenny had given Paul back his balls it could have looked like this twenty years on :

Jenny recognised that she was nagging Paul and that he was feeling like a handyman in his own house. She started to ask him more questions about what he wanted and they started to make plans and decisions together. Paul felt more involved and stayed true to his natural inclination to make Jenny happy. Jenny shared with him what made her happy, things such as hot baths, conversations, meals out, weekends away and their weekly tennis game. As Paul knew what made Jenny happy and felt in control of making her happy, he would run her a hot bath, take her out for meals and would enjoy organising the odd surprise weekend away. Although in their sixties, Paul and Jenny are a shining example of a loving relationship to all their friends and family. They lived happily ever after with Paul wearing the balls.

If Sonita had given Ahmed back his balls it could have looked like this twenty years on :

Sonita was realising that she was taking away Ahmed's masculine power by controlling the money, which meant that he had to ask her for every single penny. She felt awkward about that because it felt to her as if she was handing him his pocket money. Ahmed felt that he could never treat Sonita or surprise her or make her happy. They both became aware of the fact that the relationship wasn't working as well as it could in this format.

They identified that the fact that Sonita was handling all the finances was emasculating Ahmed. From then on, Ahmed started to control and handle the family money. He felt that he could take Sonita on little treats that made her feel good as well. He felt like a man in control of his own destiny and as he knew what was in the family kitty he could map out his vision for the future and act upon it. Because of this he purchased a stake in the company and became one of the directors and a driving force within the field. He became a role model for his two sons who he taught to manage their finances well. When they went on to university they managed to control their expenditures and they supplemented their grants by taking on weekend jobs. Sonita feels cherished, safe, taken care of and womanly and is content in her relationship with Ahmed who she adores.

They lived happily ever after with Ahmed wearing the balls.

Phoebe and Hector both realised that all was not well in their relationship. They went to a marriage counselling service and found out that Phoebe had been mothering Hector and that this was the reason that Hector was feeling increasingly dissatisfied. Phoebe felt less special to Hector than she had been at the beginning of the relationship. They went through a trial period of Phoebe treating Hector like an adult and not reminding him to put a vest on, bring his umbrella, or making him sandwiches for work. Although difficult for Phoebe with her caring nature, the results were immediate and rewarding. After three weeks both felt this worked and decided this was the way forward. Hector started to make more loving gestures towards Phoebe such as kissing her when he got home and when he left for work, instead of frowning irritatingly at his wife's attentions. He felt more like the man he was instead of feeling like an extra (naughty) child. It was a relief for him and he could see his wife more as the loving and compassionate woman she really was. This made it easier for him to be affectionate towards her and eventually more passionate and sexually attracted to her. Over the next two decades their relationship matured and blossomed. They lived happily ever after with Hector wearing the balls.

Gabriel had not realised that anything was amiss in his relationship with Judy until she cried that morning. He took time off work and they stayed in bed to talk whilst the nanny looked after the twins. He let her talk for hours and just listened until she finished. He then understood that Judy felt completely overwhelmed, exhausted, overworked and unattractive, even though she had so much help around the house. They decided that they were going to take big decisions together, with Judy consulting Gabriel any time she wanted support regardless of the size or seeming importance of the matter. Gabriel immediately felt more involved and in charge of his whole family. He felt proud that he was able to solve Judy's problem and make her feel special. Judy felt heard and instantly felt the love for her man again that had been lost during the time when she made all the decisions. They moved to Florida where they had a lovely time together raising their twins, socialising and looking forward to growing old together. Gabriel got into the habit of organising and arranging their holidays and surprising his wife. He also loved to look for and order cars for the family and got increasingly good at recognising his wife's overwhelm and taking charge at the right moment. Judy felt really supported, loved and special and she was delighted to be able to give more time to her passion of illustrating children's books. They lived happily ever after with Gabriel wearing the balls.

And what about you? Where are you in your relationship? Are you ready to give him back his balls?

Take this fun test to see if your man needs his balls back.

## QUIZ

**1. You and your man are at a barbeque together and you are thirsty. What do you do?**

a) Spot where the drinks are, walk over and pour yourself a drink or pour drinks for both of you.

b) You wait for five minutes to see if he offers to get you a drink and then give up and go and get yourself a drink.

c) You mention that you are really thirsty and know that he will get you a drink.

**2. You want to go on a Caribbean Cruise with your man. What do you do?**

a) Get half a dozen brochures from the travel agency, choose the package you like, show it to your man that evening and book it the following day.

b) Ask your man to get the brochures, you choose together and then nag him until he has booked it.

c) You mention to your man that you would so love to go on a Caribbean cruise and you don't refer to it again as you know he will surprise you with tickets on your birthday.

**3. You are at the airport with three large bags. A respectable looking man offers to give you a hand. Do you...**

a) Decline politely in your best independent-woman-of-the-world voice.

b) Say 'I think I'll manage' and struggle on, beating yourself up for turning him down.

c) You drop all the bags and exclaim, 'Thank goodness for chivalrous gentlemen!'

**4.** Your husband is having an argument with one of the children. You don't agree with his point of view and your child is crying. What do you do?

a) Jump right in, go against your husband's point of view until your child stops crying.

b) You listen for a while and then act as referee between them until they come to an agreement.

c) You go quietly about your own business, sending them lots of silent love, knowing that your husband will sort it out and your child will have learned the lesson, at the same time feeling loved and cared for.

**5.** What are you most likely to be overheard saying to your man?

a) Have you fixed the light bulb in the cellar yet? I also need you to put the rubbish out and pick Becky up from school.

b) Would you cook tonight, I'm completely exhausted.

c) Darling I'm so grateful for every day that we are together.

**6.** You walk into the theatre together. What do you look like?

a) He walks in first, looking lost, whilst you are parking the car. He waits for you before picking up the tickets.

b) You walk in together in matching outfits and you collect the tickets while he puts the coats in the cloakroom.

c) He drives up to the entrance, lets you out, gives the key to the valet parking guy, takes your arm and produces the pre-collected tickets from his inside pocket.

**7. When you think about your future together, you know:**

a) Exactly what you are going to do in ten years time because you told him at the start of your relationship what your vision was and how he would need to fit into that picture.

b) Because you sat down together and talked it through, you both know exactly what will happen. However, you still haven't told him about the third child, the Jag and the Great Dane.

c) That everything will be well because he has what it takes to get you both there.

**8. You feel like you want to make love and you don't know if your partner does too. What do you do?**

a) You tell him after dinner that tonight he is 'on' so he'd better have a shower.

b) You lie next to him in the dark and slip him a breath mint and remind him sulkily that you haven't made love in three weeks.

c) You press your body against his, whispering in his ear how wonderful he is.

9. **Your daughter comes home telling you that she wants to go to a school party. What do you advise her?**

a) To phone up the boy she fancies and ask him to take her before he gets snapped up by that brassy Brenda in the sixth form.

b) To go with a bunch of girls and dance with as many boys as possible.

c) Remind her that it is still three weeks to the dance which is plenty of time for the right guy to ask her or for her to make arrangements for her to go with a group of friends.

**Mostly A:** You have the balls. You exude mostly masculine energy in your communication with men. If you are in a relationship, it is very likely that you have been feeling dissatisfied or even frustrated and that there may be little real passion between you and your partner. Pay attention to the principles in this book if you want to transform your relationship into a loving, passionate one. If you are not in a relationship you need to focus on the content of this book in order to attract your soul mate (see chapter six).

**Mostly B:** If you are in a relationship you share custody of the balls with your man. Decide who is going to wear them and if you are prepared to give up your certainty for your happiness. If you are not in a relationship, you oscillate between masculine and feminine energies. You will not be attractive to a totally masculine man until you consistently exude more feminine energy (see chapter six) and stop taking your turn with the balls. When you give them back, give them back completely as they do not work as a security blanket. Only giving them back completely will allow a man to step up into his masculine energy unreservedly.

**Mostly C:** He wears the balls. You mostly radiate feminine energy which attracts the most masculine men. You very likely have a passionate relationship which satisfies you both in all areas. Your relationship is likely to last because this is the most natural and healthy way for the sexes to interact short and long term. Not only is this a healthy way to be in an intimate partnership but also the healthiest way to relate to the other men in your life such as your father, brother, uncles, sons, boss, employees and friends.

So now you possibly know that he needs those balls back. You may be like me and feel very comfortable wearing the balls. Why is that? Because it means that you have control over your life. It means that you do not have the fear you relate with being vulnerable. Yes, you get to go to the movies and restaurants YOU want to go to. Yes, you spend your money on things YOU choose. Yes, you raise your children YOUR way and dress your man to your OWN taste. YOUR voice is the one that is heard. You ALWAYS get to the party on time. You may THINK you are having a great relationship but IT IS AN ILLUSION!!! YOU DO NOT HAVE THE PASSIONATE RELA-TIONSHIP YOU DESERVE AND IS POSSIBLE TO HAVE!

You may wake up one day to find he is not beside you any more, having left you spiritually, emotionally or even physically. If you are really honest you know that both of you have emotionally checked out of the relationship. This is not what I want for you. I know there is another way. And you are not alone; there are hundreds and thousands of people, like you, in the same situation. They think they have to live their lives this way because relationships get less passionate over time. They think 'love wears off.' There is an easy, fun and fast way to deal with this seemingly huge and unchangeable issue.

**It is now time to give him back his balls.**

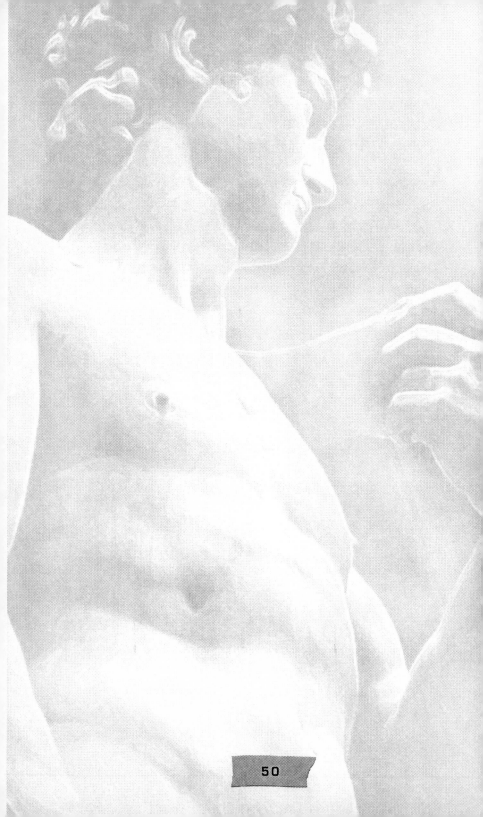

## Chapter Three
# How to give him back his balls.

Maybe you have now decided that it is necessary for changes in your relationship as things are not working. Or you have decided that it is time to change your strategies because you are not in a relationship. Or you are a parent and want to make sure that your children grow up confident in their respective energies.

Words determine how we feel. When someone asks you how you are and you reply 'I feel great,' you automatically feel better than you would have felt when you said 'Not bad.'

Some words are predominantly used by feminine women and some are used by women who have a tendency to go more into their masculine energy.

The first step to giving him back his balls is by examining and changing your use of language.

Words that are used more by women and men operating from feminine energy include:

Wonder
Magic
Treasure
Feel
Chat

Love
Yes
Beautiful
Please
Maybe

Words that are used more by women and men operating from masculine energy include:

Must
Never
Focus
Know
Prove
No
Do
Now
Action
Done

Which words would you tend to use more often? Your husband or boyfriend? Your son?

| Phrases used more by women and men who operate from feminine energy: | Phrases used more by women and men who operate from masculine energy: |
|---|---|
| I've changed my mind | I never go back on my word |
| I'll see how I feel | I'll think about it |

| | |
|---|---|
| Thank you | Great! |
| That is beautiful | That is interesting |
| I love that | I like it |
| We have a magic between us | We have a good relationship |
| He's so good to me, he's my king | We keep each other on our toes |
| Oh that's so cute | That's nice |
| I'm hungry | Let's eat |
| We're out of food | Can you do the grocery shopping |
| Dinner's ready | Come to the table now |
| The car's broken down | I'll phone the garage to get the car fixed |
| I've run out of money | Let me take some money out of the cash point |
| Darling, the headmaster phoned | I have sorted things out with the headmaster |
| I trust that you will sort it out | The solution to this is... |
| I'd love a new sofa | I have ordered a new sofa |

| | |
|---|---|
| I would like to go out for a meal | I've booked a table for 8pm |
| You're the best | What did you do that for? |
| My man is my rock | The old man is Ok |
| Honey take me | Come on, let's go |
| That's ok, maybe we can do it tomorrow | How could you be so stupid as to forget? |

Circle the phrase in each pair that you are more likely to use. What about your spouse? Your Dad? Nephew?

Do you get it? Listen to yourself and listen to others. What type of words and phrases do they use? You will soon get the idea and be able to tell whether someone operates from masculine or feminine energy.

Start catching yourself and use the more feminine version of the two possibilities. If you are new to this type of language it might seem that you are behaving like a doormat.

If I say 'Dinner's ready,' he will never come to the table if he is used to hearing me yell 'Come to the table now.' If I say 'I've run out of money,' I could be waiting an eternity before he would give me any. At least when I say 'I need money' or 'I've ordered a new sofa,' I can be certain that I'll get it.

You are so used to the certainty and control that the old language patterns have given you, that you are unable to see the possibility of the new. It may take some time and practice but it is definitely worth it.

Of course in an emergency, you may need to be very direct. 'Johnny is drowning!' versus 'Darling, wouldn't it be lovely if Johnny had not fallen in the river' is obviously preferable.

Here are some stories from my coaching business to illustrate how using new, feminine language works better for everyone.

My client Jean was married to Mike, an astute young man. He had a degree from the London Business School and had just ventured out into a new business. He was stepping out into unknown territory. Jean was a petite and gorgeous blonde who was able to hold her own in any situation. She could walk into a room with confidence. She knew she could handle any situation. Jean told me that Mike was totally committed to his new venture but most of the time would ask her for advice. They also had a new baby and Jean had temporarily exchanged her usual career for that of full-time mother, which she thoroughly enjoyed. She came to coaching because she felt that she was giving Mike too much advice which made her tired and increasingly resentful. She felt very unwomanly since she had their little one and felt that besides a milk bar she was a nappy changing and feeding machine. Mike was so engrossed in building his business and was so tired at night, that he did not even mention going out in the evenings. Jean felt imprisoned by her circumstances and she felt that she was not only running the household but also acting as an advisor for Mike's new business. She felt that she was wearing the balls in the relationship. We worked on giving Mike back his balls.

Jean consciously changed the words and phrases she used. Slowly things changed. She was flabbergasted when she used the sentence 'Darling, I am sure you will sort it out' instead of her usual offering of a solution. After an initial whining session, Mike straightened himself out, took a deep breath and regained his focus. 'Sure I will' he smiled. The following day he told Jean about his solution for the previous day's challenge.

At our next appointment Jean told me that she had thought it would not work to start with and how encouraged she was when it did. She has since used this phrase frequently and many others with the same positive effect.

Another client was Doreen, a high powered executive who dressed in business suits, wore glasses and a very smart bobbed haircut. Doreen worked in a bank. She had just started dating Jimmy, a good looking man with 'hunk like' features who worked as a sculptor. She initially met Jimmy when she was invited to an exhibition her painter friend had organised and was blown away by the masterpieces he had produced. When she met the creator, she was even more impressed and they had ended up talking for hours. It seemed she had known him all her life and the feeling was mutual. They had gone on a few dates and there was definitely chemistry between them but Doreen found that she mostly took the lead. She would always say things such as 'Come on, let's go to the movies' and 'I think we should eat at La Scala.' She felt that lately Jimmy made less advances towards her and wondered why. I suggested that she change her language to sound like this; 'Honey take me' and 'I'd love to go somewhere new' and 'I'm hungry.' She gave these a try over the next two weeks. At first she felt really awkward and scared. If anyone from work could have heard her, they would have thought she was nuts. These were phrases she had never used before. She gave them a go and even though in the beginning she felt she did not get through to Jimmy at all, she persisted and was pleasantly surprised that Jimmy started to respond by taking the lead.

I also worked with Annie, a lovely lady from Indonesia who had been in the county for twenty years. Annie was in her late forties and she had not lost any of the stunning looks she must have had as a young woman. She had been married to Adam for the last decade. Adam had built his own house and when he met Annie, he was a successful real estate developer. Annie was a teacher in the local dance school. She was gracious, elegant and beautiful. It seemed she had it all. When she came to me for coaching, she confided that she had become critical of Adam over the last few years. Together we found that she would often ask him the rhetorical question, 'What did you do that for?' both in private and public.

She changed to saying 'You're the best' and meaning it any time she felt the old question coming up. In the beginning she felt this was particularly inauthentic but as she saw the huge impact this had on both Adam's responses and her own feelings, she was committed to saying these words and eventually became hooked on them. The meaning of the words, 'You're the best' really started to ring true for her as Adam, encouraged by his wife's new use of words, began to perform accordingly.

Are you ready to give the new language a go? I expect that in the beginning it will feel as inauthentic as it did to Annie. I believe that you will feel just as awkward as Doreen and you might be just as flabbergasted at the results as Jean was. You have everything to gain and nothing to lose. The only things you have got to lose are balls. Balls that were never really yours in the first place.

Look at one word that you would like to change.

For example you might like to change the word 'think' for 'feel' because the word 'think' means that you are operating more from your head, which is a masculine trait, whereas 'feel' represents the heart, which is a more feminine place from which to operate. If you frequently use the sentence 'Let me think about it' you may want to substitute it with 'I will let you know how I feel about that.'

Or you might like to change the word 'must' for the word 'want' as the word 'must' is very directive and evokes the reaction of resistance, whereas the word 'want' implies choice. If you use the word 'must' in your relationship with your man, such as 'You must put the rubbish out,' he will feel ordered about and resentful whereas if you say 'I want the rubbish cleared,' he will feel that he makes you happy when he chooses to complete this task.

Words only represent 7% of communication but what about other components as:

Your posture, your movements, gestures and facial expressions which can either be more feminine or more masculine.

## FEMININE AND MASCULINE POSTURES

### Standing

**Feminine:** knees soft, one knee slightly bent, weight on straighter leg, legs and torso slightly twisted from central core, one hip pushed out higher than the other, arms bent, one or two hands touching the body or clothing, head slightly tilted.

**Masculine:** standing upright with locked knees, straight elbows, chest up and out, head facing front and not tilted, chin slightly up, feet planted shoulder-width apart. When Rex dressed up like a woman (yes, a huge 6' 5" one with coarse features and very obviously a man in drag) for fun to welcome the Aussie navy to Jakarta, he found himself caught up in the role and adopted very gracious, exaggerated feminine moves and postures. After everyone had had a couple of drinks he was pursued by all.

## Sitting

**Feminine:** legs crossed at ankle or knee, knees slightly bent and close together, weight often on one buttock, hands touching each other or another body part, head tilted.

**Masculine:** legs wide apart, feet firmly planted on ground, hands firmly on knees, arms out showing definitive angle at elbow, body straight on, head un-tilted.

## FEMININE AND MASCULINE MOVES

## Walking

**Feminine:** small steps, swaying hips, light gait, swinging arms, head glancing from side to side, dance-like quality to movement, more moseying and undirected.

**Masculine:** larger steps, feet flatter, static hips and shoulders, head facing front, marching quality to movement, more direct.

If a woman walks like a man she rips her pencil skirt. That is how a man in drag gives himself away. When Rex borrowed my tight skirt for the Aussie navy, his biggest challenge was to take small enough steps to keep the skirt intact.

## FEMININE AND MASCULINE GESTURES

**Feminine:** hand limp, rounded, flowing quality to movements, open palms, points with entire hand, gestures are playful and fluttery, soft touch of body.

**Masculine:** hand strong, jerking punchy quality to movements, closed fists, points with a jabbing finger, gestures forceful and definite, hard thumps to body.

## FEMININE AND MASCULINE FACIAL EXPRESSIONS

**Feminine:** facial muscles softened, more smiles, eyes wide open, lips slightly parted, eyebrows lifted, head moving and tilting gently.

**Masculine:** facial muscles taut, smiling mostly for specific reasons, eyes more narrowed and darting about, lips closed, jaw firm, eyebrows lowered, head moving purposefully in single movements.

When asked to rate a line of women on attraction, those who smile get the highest ratings, even above those who would be rated as classical beauties.

Take on one small thing at a time. Practice having your

lips constantly slightly parted rather than having them tight together. You will find it makes you feel softer and more feminine and people will approach you in a different manner. This one small change can make a huge difference. My client Doreen (mentioned previously) started by transforming her language and soon after her gestures also became more flowing and rounded, she smiled more and found that Jimmy found her more attractive and she had less tension headaches.

You will find that you need some practice first and I suggest you have some fun with it and pretend you are a new film star or model walking down your local high street. Note the differences in your own sensation and people's reaction to you. As a man, use more of the masculine moves, postures and gestures. Pretend to be Arnie in a new movie or Sly Stallone on the prowl. The number one organising principle is to have fun whilst you try these new suggestions. You may want to walk down the High Street in a more feminine way and walk back in a more masculine way.

Let us talk clothes for a moment. Clothes maketh the man and of course the woman too.

Do you find that the clothes you wear are largely androgynous? When buying clothes ask yourself 'Is this something my man (or a man) could wear?' If the answer is 'Yes' or 'Yes if it was in a bigger size' then DO NOT BUY IT.

What makes an outfit feminine and what makes an outfit masculine?

Feminine Clothes

Complex

Detailed

Fussy

Aesthetic

Flimsy

Colourful

Soft

Light

Playful

Snuggly

Shows off shape

Unique

Wavy

Masculine Clothes

Simple

Plain

Functional

Hard-wearing

Monotone

Rough

Heavy

Serious

Protective

Structured

Uniform

Some women have to wear fairly uniform, masculine type of clothing at work. Other women have the opportunity to wear feminine clothing but feel awkward because they have been dressing androgynously for so long. A great way to ease into the new way of dressing is to buy yourself some pretty and sexy lingerie and wear this under your normal clothing. Only you (and possibly one other!) know what lies beneath and this will make you feel more feminine.

Men's shoes are flat, functional, chunky and usually dark. This is so that the man can stand planted and flat on the ground. Traditionally men have needed to be able to stand their ground, defend their women and chase game. When a woman wears 'mens' shoes' her gait tends to be flat footed, she takes bigger steps, sways her hips less and her legs seem shorter. Strangely it is socially accepted worldwide for women to wear men's shoes and yet a man in woman's shoes is presumed gay or off to a fancy dress stag night. I remember vividly the large and hairy gentleman, dressed as a fairy who checked in at Gatwick airport in front of me on a flight to Amsterdam. All the airport staff giggled, smiled or laughed out loud. When a woman in hiking boots and wearing hunting gear checked in behind me, not a single person batted an eyelid.

Womens' shoes tend to have higher heels, be impractical, pretty, any colour (preferably a bright one) and co-ordinated with the rest of their outfit.

You might say that you will never wear shoes that hurt and deform your feet. A good way to get into wearing feminine shoes is to wear the sensible ones to get you to where you need to go and then change into the stunning ones once you have reached your destination. There are plenty of shoes that look pretty and feminine and are comfortable too. It just takes some shopping around. A lot of us are just in the habit of wearing certain types of shoes all the time without thinking about it. If you are committed to becoming more of the feminine woman that you already are, I assure you that it's worth investing some time, thought and money into this area.

Well-applied make-up in everyday life embodies femininity. Too much make-up can look harsh and counteract the effect you are going for. It may look masculine if you draw harsh outlines, or have foundation plastered on. Make-up needs to be used to enhance the good features that you have.

The importance of jewelry and accessories such as scarves, hair ornaments, bracelets, earrings, rings anklets, brooches, belts, bags and hats is to accentuate and enhance your femininity. An outfit can look completely bland but with accessories and jewelry, you can transform it into something very feminine.

### Feminine and masculine accessories

**Feminine:** diamonds, small sparkly rings, thin gold, detailed bracelets, pretty pendants, frilly hair accessories, beautiful floaty scarves, decorative hats, ornamental belts, dangling ear rings, impractical and lots of bags (that have smaller bags inside them).

**Masculine:** Big, solid rings, thick gold or silver chains, a minimum of jewelry, functional belts to keep up trousers rather than to accentuate waistline, warm and thick scarves for heat retention, protective hats in dark colours to add character, thick gloves or leather gloves with large stitching.

Women's accessories can be flimsy whereas men's first priority tends to be function. If a man wears a pendant it is usually drawing attention to the hairy and fit chest he is proud of. When a woman wears a pendant it is usually to draw attention to her cleavage (which is hopefully hair-free).

The activities we partake in can also give the impression of being more masculine than feminine.

We can conduct sports activities in either a feminine or masculine mode.

Feminine mode : detached from the outcome of winning, more there for team and social aspects, doing sports for aesthetic reasons (to get a good looking body), to feel good, to be with nature, for fun, to encourage others to stay in shape, to glow, to become connected to our bodies and the elements.

Masculine mode : to compete, to win, to be special and unique, to excel, to push yourself beyond the limits, to be a mean, lean fighting machine, to bulk up and build muscle for an endorphin kick, to show others what you are made of and how it's done, as an escape from pressures as with an energy valve.

All sports can be conducted in either mode. However there are sports in which it is easier to feel feminine such as dancing, ice-skating, synchronised swimming, aqua aerobics, aerobics, yoga, Pilates, T'ai-chi, walking, netball, rounders, volley ball, boules, rhythmic gymnastics, social skiing, dressage and hot air ballooning.

There are sports in which it is easier to feel masculine , for instance rugby, speed skating, point-to-point horse riding, lane swimming, sprinting, gymnastics rings, boxing, kung fu, basketball, American football, slalom racing, speedway, speed boating, grand prix and parachuting.

If you are currently partaking in sports that do not feel good to you, it can be that the activity you have chosen is too singular and masculine. I used to be a successful internationally competitive Ironman tri-athlete. An Ironman race consists of a 2.8 mile swim, a 118 mile bike ride and a 26.1 mile run, all in one day. To start with I felt really great, training outdoors, being with nature and feeling my body tone up. When I became more competitive I started to enjoy the process less and less and felt it became a chore that I no longer gained pleasure from. I met only a few women in the sport who kept their femininity and were able to consistently perform at a high level. A great role model was the American professional Ironman Triathlete Wendy Ingram, who manages to win an Ironman race and appear fresh as a daisy and radiantly feminine the day after. I personally needed to be away from this level of intensity and stopped the training and competitions.

Now I run, cycle and swim for fun, simply because it makes me feel good. I also dance, practice yoga, T'ai-chi and Pilates which entails smaller, more flowing movements. Whatever sport or physical activity you choose, make sure that you honour yourself as a woman and take into account adding some feminine ingredients to the way you take part in them. Using music can aid to feel more feminine whatever the sport.

Creative and practical activities like painting, singing, sewing, house cleaning, DIY, gardening, cooking etc. can also be partaken in a feminine or masculine way. If you cook a meal in a feminine way you will more likely work intuitively adding unlisted ingredients. Even if you follow a recipe, your focus will be more on how it looks and tastes and how much you enjoy the process rather than on achieving a definite outcome. It's not a big tragedy if the scrambled eggs turn into an omelet somewhere along the way. If you were tapped into mainly masculine energy you would probably be working to time-limits, be organised and follow a recipe to the letter. For men, cooking tends to be more about the scientific measurable principle involved than the pleasure and art it tends to be for women. They are more focused on outcome rather than enjoying the process.

Task:

Choose two activities over the next ten days that you want to conduct in a more feminine way. Keep a journal and write down what you are going to do and keep regular tabs on what you have experienced, how it makes you feel different, how the outside world reacts, how men in general react and specifically if you have a partner, how he reacts.

Use this fun checklist to measure your progress in the areas we have discussed in this chapter.

| | Very feminine | Masculine/ feminine mix | Very masculine |
|---|---|---|---|
| Words | | | |
| Phrases | | | |
| Posture | | | |
| Movements | | | |
| Gestures | | | |
| Facial Expressions | | | |
| Clothes | | | |
| Shoes | | | |
| Make-up | | | |
| Accessories | | | |
| Physical activities | | | |
| Creative activities | | | |
| Practical activities | | | |

You can copy this list or print it off the website **www.brigittesumner.com**

Keep doing these exercises until you are completely relaxed in your feminine energy. Reclaiming your femininity is the first step in giving your man back his balls and/or attracting a masculine man into your life. Whatever strategies you choose, follow through for at least twenty one days. It takes twenty one days to form a habit. You will find that you are able to remind yourself on a less regular basis after that time. To permanently shed those balls you need to remind yourself that you are a feminine woman without balls. It may be that under stress you easily grab for the balls again! People tend to regress to old behavioural patterns under stress. Just bear that in mind and be easy on yourself. Most people are hard on themselves and easy on others. We beat ourselves up for slipping, for not being perfect and for making mistakes.

Remember, mistakes are really learning experiences. When an airplane flies from London to New York, it is on the precise route for only 3% of the time, yet it still gets to New York. The pilot does not get depressed because he is a few degrees off route. He will look at his instruments, find out that he is a few degrees off course and correct it. Some time later, he will look again, find out that he is now a couple of degrees off course to the other side and correct it again. At no time will he feel the urge to don his parachute and eject himself from the plane. Even though the plane that takes you to New York is only on the exact route for 3% of the time, you will still get there. Apply this analogy to this and other areas of your life that you intend to change. What that means is that when you slip up or make a mistake, you do not sink into a depression. You do not whine and whinge as if the worst has happened. No, you get up, ruffle your feathers, pull yourself up by the bra straps and get on with it!

We are now ready to explore the next vital steps.

Note: Femininity is a state of confidence in who you are and must never be mistaken for subservience, cowering or accepting any form of abuse. Men who operate from true masculine energy do not use this to abuse women.

## Chapter Four
# Give him back his balls in the bedroom

One place a man really needs his balls is in the bedroom, and what I mean specifically is when you are making love. Sex with a ball-less man is not exciting for a feminine woman. Sex between partners who hold joint custody of the balls is like an intimate cuddling session gone too far, without huge passion.

Sex with a masculine man makes a woman feel that he can take her to total ecstasy. In doing so repeatedly he makes her happy which fulfills her completely. There is passion, excitement, which can drive you crazy, makes you wild, makes you lose yourself and he remains very much in charge.

That doesn't mean that there is only one way to have sex, since we as women need variety and sometimes what sent us orgasmic yesterday might leave us cold today. When sex has great polarity, you can lose yourself as you trust that he will protect you and not hurt you as you totally surrender to his power. He is willing to explore and he knows what you want or is eager to find out.

On the other hand, sex with a ball-less man (one living in his feminine energy) is not as exciting for a feminine woman. He will take less control, probably frequently and nervously ask 'Is that OK?' and will not take charge.

He might even expect her to do all the work, repeatedly, and be more focused on his own pleasure. Over time, your sex life can become staid and routine.

If a woman constantly takes the lead in bed this makes a man feel incompetent, under pressure to perform, lazy and can lead to impotence.

It can make her feel that this is yet another area in which she has to take control and do all the work, which can make her feel even more exhausted and resentful.

Most of the time, women need foreplay in order to warm up slowly and be ready to receive their partner fully. Typically, men are ready in an instant. As soon as he has an erection he is ready to penetrate you, whereas you might not be ready for another half an hour. You can look at it this way: A woman is like an old-fashioned charcoal barbeque where it takes a lot of fuel and a long time before the device is ready to start cooking. A man is like a modern gas barbeque where you flick the switch and it's ready to go in an instant.

It can be agonising for a man to carry out long-term foreplay because he doesn't need it and wants to get to the point of ejaculation as quickly as possible to release the massive build up of sexual energy. For him, five minutes of foreplay will seem like hours, whereas for you it will seem like seconds.

Let's think back to our medieval couple Angus and Isobel. One of her expected duties was to fulfill Angus' sexual needs. Sex was probably more satisfying for him than for her. He was probably not attuned to her needs and did not know much about foreplay. She would be content with the occasional quickie but might have been dissatisfied with a constant menu of sex that was over almost before she knew it had started. He might have hurt her in the process as he was disconnected from her needs.

For our 1970s couple Felicity and Richard, sex was very likely to quickly have become a matter of routine that was not as exciting and fun as it could have been. The intellectual and social attractions between them were probably stronger than the sexual attractions. They may have gone without sex for extended periods of time, neither of them needing that close physical connection. Because each of them was both feminine and masculine, neither of them needed the other party to complement their energy and fill them up.

They may have found other ways to fill the need for connection such as focusing on the children, Richard focusing on his spirituality and Felicity being superwoman whilst he's gone. These are all distractions from the real problem. A couple like this could be overheard to say: 'I'd rather read a good book than have sex.'

When a woman claims that chocolate is better than sex, people may laugh but it's not very funny because it is probably an indication that her sex life doesn't fulfill her due to she and her partner having similar energies. This may lead to comfort eating, overindulgence in food, cigarettes, alcohol, TV watching, flirting with co-workers and any other number of seemingly harmless activities. These can all have negative consequences as they can make you overweight, unhealthy and mask the real problem which is disconnection from your partner stemming from lack of polarity.

My coaching client Lisa came to me, desperate because of her weight issue. She was married to Steve. They were living in a pretty, dreamy little cottage in a country village and they had two teenage children. Lisa and Steve were buzzing, busy, happy and content. Steve had his own wholesale food business and Lisa was still at home looking after the children who did not really need her continuous presence and attention any more. She was dabbling with aromatherapy and Indian head massage courses but was unsure which route to pursue. When she consulted me she was 5 stone overweight. Her doctor told her she really needed to lose weight as her heart was getting overloaded by the extra weight, putting her at risk of heart disease.

We found out that although Lisa and Steve seemed happy, Lisa was wearing the balls and was the driving force in the marriage, even in the bedroom. In fact, the amount of times that Lisa and Steve had sex in the last year could be counted on one hand. Lisa had found a nice substitute for her need to connect to herself and the world in eating. It started when the children were small, when it seemed such a waste to throw out whatever they had not eaten from their plate and moved on to eating the last biscuits in the pack too. She would sit on the sofa after a few hours of housework and watch training videos whilst drinking fizzy drinks and eating chocolate biscuits. She ballooned gradually and steadily. As Lisa sat in my office clutching a handful of tear-drenched tissues, she exclaimed that she could not go on this way any longer! I could have easily given Lisa a diet sheet and told her to come back next week and we would have found out after months of fruitless coaching meetings that there was little or no progress. Instead, we found that there was a direct link between her eating challenges and the fact that she was so much in her masculine energy. She told me she had taken charge of everything as Steve was too busy with his work. Over the years she had started to feel contempt and disgust for her man. At parties she would either speak of him scathingly or with embarrassment. She was in charge of their well-oiled household and was sick and tired of being alone in this task. She was the one who arranged the children's hobbies, schools and other activities. Steve was not even aware of which school his children attended. Lisa would organise holidays, pack for the family and be the driving force of whatever was left of their social life. She was obviously wearing the balls and feeling empty. The eating made her feel full and this numbed and masked her feelings of desperation. Lisa had come to the conclusion that she either wanted to separate from Steve or something drastic had to happen. Her biggest realisation that she needed to change came when Kayleigh, her fourteen year old daughter had started to have weight issues also. Lisa realised that she was not a great role model for her daughter, and was determined to make changes. During the appointments that followed, I gave Lisa homework which gradually resulted in giving Steve back his balls. She started to use much more feminine words and language such as 'want' versus 'must' and thanking Steve for every little thing he did. This was not easy and Lisa resented this approach for a few weeks. But after a while she saw that this reinforced Steve's few contributions to the household chores. It also focused Lisa's attention on the fact that he did actually do things around the house, something that she had stopped noticing long ago. The next piece of homework was for her to find different ways to fill herself up than food. She started to take long hot baths with aromatherapy, enjoy a weekly massage and have regular manicures, pedicures and facials. This made her glow and feel special and much more feminine. Steve started to notice this new found equilibrium and glow that reminded him of when he first met her. He noticed the lovely wafts of lavender she seemed to be enveloped in lately and was charmed by the new ways in which she moved and used different words. These woke up his dormant nether regions. By this time her homework was to zip her lips and sit on her hands. She did and waited, even when it became uncomfortable. She waited far beyond the stage she would have waited ever before. Eventually Steve made a pass and they had their first steamy bedroom session for years. Both of them were overcome by the passion they felt for one another. From then on, Steve seduced his wife more often, which made Lisa feel so special, wanted, womanly and desired. Her need for food to fill her up diminished and she started to shed the weight. Steve, encouraged by what he had accomplished in the bedroom, took more charge of tasks within the family and eventually was back in control of the family's destiny. Lisa felt totally feminine and once more adored her husband. When at parties, she spoke admiringly about him to her two jealous 'friends,' who had been looking forward to Lisa's messy divorce. They lived happily ever after with Steve wearing the balls.

When a woman or a man says that they are just not interested in sex, they are really saying that they are unhappy. Sex is a primary need and is an inherent part of being human although some choose celibacy as an option. You will notice that when you start giving him back his balls the appetite for sex will be rekindled for both of you.

I would like to introduce you to Laura and Mark, our modern day couple. Laura is a stunningly beautiful woman in her thirties with long black hair. She runs a health spa for women. Mark is in his early forties and has short dark hair and striking features. He works in his father's investment business. Mark is devoted to Laura and their two lovely young children and they have an excellent relationship. Laura is confident, outspoken and gregarious and behaves, moves, speaks and dresses in a very feminine way. Mark is a sensitive, polite, humourous and totally masculine man. He dresses, speaks, behaves and conducts himself in masculine ways. The two of them have an active, exciting, and totally fulfilling sex life. Mark is fully aware of what excites his woman, what turns her on and how to pleasure her in many different ways. Over the years the sex between them has got better, as they both have taken time to explore the other's body and convey their likes and dislikes in bed, in a loving way. There have been times when either of them has misunderstood the other, such as just after the birth of their children because Laura was so engrossed and seemingly totally fulfilled with her babies that Mark thought she was not interested in sex. As their communication channels stayed open and both of them were able to stay in their respective masculine and feminine energies, they soon found out what was bothering their lover and were eager to remedy the situation.

So what does a night of love-making look like for this magnetically charged couple?

They start by hiring a babysitter and going out for a romantic candlelit dinner in the local Thai restaurant. He orders some dishes which he knows she will enjoy and the chance he takes on the choice of wine really pays off. They talk in a leisurely and unhurried way avoiding talking about household problems and issues at Mark's work. Mark frequently takes Laura's hand and they have long moments of simply gazing into each others eyes with neither feeling the need to say anything.

They have a little cuddle in the car on the way home, where Mark slips his hand under Laura's sleek top. He pulls her close to him at a traffic light and kisses her deeply and tenderly. When the light turns to green Laura places her head on Mark's shoulder and rests her hand in his lap, gently caressing his groin area.

Having parked the car in their driveway, Mark gives his wife an unhurried, lengthy kiss and whispers lovingly in her ear. The children are already in bed and the babysitter drives herself home. Mark sweeps Laura up in his arms and carries her to the bedroom where he places her on the bed. One of the children wakes up and starts crying. Mark takes charge, reassuring the child and getting her back to sleep. He returns to his wife and kisses and holds her once more. When he senses that she is ready he teases her and starts to take her clothes off very slowly drinking her in with his eyes. He tells her how beautiful she looks and how much he wants her. He continues to take the lead and assesses what she is feeling and how ready she is while at no time turning into a weak 'pleaser' or an unfeeling beast. At all times he is also fully in touch with his own needs and is able to guide her gently towards what feels great for both of them. She totally surrenders and allows herself to be vulnerable and to be taken and seduced by her husband. At no time does she feel that she has to do something that is uncomfortable to her. She doesn't give any directions in bed as Mark knows through their great communication over time what her likes and dislikes are, what turns her on and what her signs of discomfort and pleasure are.

I'm sure you can just imagine how this unfolds and this occasion is representative of Laura and Mark's love life when in their natural state.

**6 TIPS FOR GIVING YOUR MAN BACK HIS BALLS IN THE BEDROOM.**

1. Let him take the lead. He needs to provide you with direction even though that may feel awkward in the beginning. This means that you must wait for him to approach you, be it in your long term relationship or with a man you have only met recently. It is good to get into this habit even before you start to go out with someone. Let him chase you, do not chase him as the chasing is his part of the game. He needs to be able to seduce you in order to feel his 'win'. In bed, if he has not taken the lead, you may want to take his hand and gently guide him, or whisper in his ear to ask for what you want. It makes your man feel that he is in control of what makes you happy. He will feel that he is in charge, which is what he is about. You will feel like a princess, totally being taken care of. This will ensure that the relationship stays healthy with your man being the go getter and you being able to relax in your feminine energy. You will find that life will seem so much more effortless when you are in your feminine energy in your intimate relationship.

2. Trust that he has your best interests at heart. Provided that you have made a good choice of partner, he will have your best interests at heart and will want to please you and make you happy. He wants to make you feel good, he wants to make you happy and his bedroom mission is to give you pleasure, feel connected with you, make you feel safe, special and loved during sexual intercourse. You must let go of any anxiety and wish to keep control, as that will stop you from completely giving over to the waves of ecstasy and you will need to trust. As this may be new to both of you, he may mess up to start with. This does not mean he can't be trusted. It means he is learning. You will need to let him know what is working and what is not working. He will feel closer to you and more connected when you do this. He will feel that he can make you feel safe and is an expert on what turns you on (men love to be experts). When you start trusting him in the bedroom, you will find that you can trust him in other areas also. You will be able to give him back his balls on other fronts.

3. Lie back, surrender, relax and enjoy yourself. Once you have started to trust, remember to enjoy what he is doing. This is your time to totally give over to your emotions and feelings and ride the waves of pleasure. This will make your man feel like a hero, he is the one who has achieved this and to him it will feel like a major win. It will make him feel like he invented orgasms! You will be able to relearn the pleasure of just surrendering to feeling great.

4. Be honest. Be honest with yourself first of all. Have you been totally fulfilled or just been focusing on his satisfaction? If the latter, you need to decide your feeling good is just as important and that is the only thing you can control. Don't fake an orgasm or any kind of pleasure you are not feeling and especially do not pretend that you feel pleasure when you are really feeling pain. Any time you feign a headache because you have had difficulty to unwind from work, you are not being honest and it is preferable to ask 'I don't know why, but I don't feel in the mood for sex, can we have a cuddle instead?'

Let him know what really turns you on and what does not. If you find this difficult, because he has been using a particular position or technique for years and you have never said anything, you may want to say something along these lines: "Why don't we try xyz tonight, it's just a fun something I saw in a woman's magazine". This makes him feel that you are taking an interest and want to make this important part of your relationship work. It reassures him that you will not complain later on down the line. You will feel that you have nothing to hide, your vulnerability becomes your strength because there is only truth and the truth is stronger than anything else. There is no more nonsense and nothing can come between you.

5. Go with the flow. Let go of any attachment to the outcome and go with whatever comes up and feels natural and good. So often we are mentally attached to

images of how it should go. From movies and books we have pictures of the ideal scenario. This flowing allows your man to ride the feminine energy. Because men are so rigid in their movements and energy, they crave and need to have the flow of our femininity and they can finally let go. They need the polar opposite. The Yang needs the Yin, the summer needs the winter, the sun needs the moon and the positive needs the negative. When you go with the flow, you let go of control and feel relaxed and un-frustrated. It makes your bond strong, balanced and resilient. You will feel that your relationship can take beatings as it will bend rather than break in high winds.

6. Receive compliments beautifully. Learn and get into the habit of receiving compliments about yourself. Most of us are very uncomfortable when people pay us a compliment and we wave it away. Accept a compliment about any part of yourself. The easiest way is just by saying 'thank you.' When your man tells you you have a beautiful body, just say 'Thank you, enjoy it' instead of saying 'but don't look at my stretch marks' or 'well, you haven't seen me naked yet!' Many women make the mistake of feeling that they have to pay him a compliment in return, 'you have great legs too' just does not work! When you accept his compliments in the bedroom he feels confident as he is not made to feel wrong and it encourages him to pay you more compliments and look for what is great about you. Once you are used to it and silence that voice in your head, you will blossom and appreciate

his flattering remarks. Your relationship will turn into one of mutual respect and admiration.

**6 WAYS TO ENSURE YOU STAY WEARING HIS BALLS in the bedroom**

1. Order him about. Tell him when he is expected to turn up for your bedroom romp. What he is supposed to wear and not to wear. Where to put his leg, 'not there, idiot!', 'now give me....' Push and shove him disrespectfully.

2. Complain and criticise. Tell him what he is doing wrong and what does not work. Moan about it endlessly. 'Darling, when you put your tongue in my ear, it feels like a dog licking me.' 'We never have sex any more!'

3. Perform in order to get a result. Dress a particular way, in sexy underwear, not to make you feel feminine for both of your pleasure, but to manipulate him to get your own way. Moan so loudly that you are almost convincing yourself that you are having a good time. Only put on the show when you want or need something from him.

4. Be too distracted by your career. Work late nights and have endless meetings. Bring your work home or work from home and never stop. Take phone calls during sex.

5. Make your children or your social life more important than intimacy with your man. Arrange something for

every night of the week without him. Have your bed-room door open, so that your children have access to you at all hours.

6. Compete with him 'Race ya!' Rush to get to orgasm first and claim victory over your man. Constantly have the last word, strive to look the best, have more excit-ing ideas and new positions than him.

My clients have found that once they were beyond the initial stage of finding the 'homework' awkward, they started to love it and find new ways to integrate these new and exciting ways of deeply connecting with their partner. They were starting to enjoy their sex life. Over the next few weeks they found that it worked to watch certain types of TV programmes and not others. The soap opera's with the characters that for the sake of the script cannot be honest, committed and loving are bad examples and poor role models of how to live a fulfilled intimate life. Better programs to watch are films such as 'Sleepless in Seattle,' 'Bridges of Madison County,' 'You've got mail,' 'Bringing down the house,' etc. These are great examples of stories where the man happily wears or finds his balls and the women surrender into their femininity. If you spend the majority of your social time with couples who are in each others' energy, you will very likely start to act like them and imperceptibly start to do the same. When you find couples who are both comfortable in their own energy and you socialise with them, you will notice that it will be easier to remain each in your own natural energies.

When it seems that no positive change is occurring, realise that this can take time. Give yourselves permission to screw up and laugh about it. Use all the suggestions in this and other chapters to enhance your femininity and allow him to fully feel the amazing power of his own masculine sexual energy.

## Chapter Five
# How to Give him back his balls as the family leader

Historically, the man was the leader of the family, the one to determine the destiny of his little unit and the one who would hold the vision of the family.

In our medieval couple, Angus and Isobel, Angus knew what he wanted to achieve in his lifetime, what was expected from him and what the future of his sons and daughter would be like. Isobel had a very good understanding of what that looked like as there were only a limited amount of options available to people who were born in that particular era and under those particular circumstances. There was not much choice available. Angus was driven by his vision and pursued his goals himself without sharing them with his wife. He certainly would not have asked Isobel for her opinion or advice. 'We are considering to go hunting on Friday, Isobel, darling, does that fit in with your plans? Or would you prefer me to stay home and look after the bairns?' would not have been something to be heard in their household. It is likely that he revealed his ambitions in life to his own father and Isobel's father when asking for her hand in marriage. He possibly shared his visions, ambitions and goals with his brothers, his friends and when considered to be old enough to be told, his sons.

Our 1970's couple, Richard and Felicity had decided upon and discussed their shared goals and vision for the future at length, and both of them had agreed to take their equal share in achieving their long term goals. When Richard went to India to find his life's purpose, Felicity naturally took over the responsibility of holding their vision and making strides towards their shared goals. When Felicity was in Canada for her research project, it was Richard who went forward and made progress towards their communal aspirations. One of their goals was to move house after the girls had both gone to university and build a house in the countryside to start a smallholding with ducks, geese, chickens and a few goats. Richard would take early retirement, and Felicity would do some more research projects abroad. She really enjoyed her time in Canada, made a lot of new friends and felt that she learned a lot. She felt that she was challenged to solve problems, which she loved. At times our couple did not necessarily have any particular goals or aspirations as is the same with many modern day couples.

## What is a vision?

A vision is a dream, a non-visible goal or series of goals set in the future that are either written down or contained within one's thinking. People are excited to achieve their vision at some stage in life. A vision keeps us motivated to move forward and stay on track even through adversity. When there is a big enough 'why', the 'what' and the 'how' will follow.

For example, it can be an eight year old boy's vision to be playing tennis at Wimbledon when he is eighteen. He can get excited about going to his daily tennis coaching, by envisioning himself playing at Wimbledon centre court. He may fantasise about hearing the referee, seeing the ball boys running around to pick up the stray tennis balls and feeling the wind and the sun on his face when he has made his dream a reality. Having this vision will ensure he will not be deterred by boredom, the bad weather and frustration with tennis partners during the many, long and seemingly unsuccessful years to come.

Some modern day couples do not have a vision for the future. It may be that the woman expects her man to hold a vision for them as a couple. It may be that the man has lost his balls somewhere during his life and expects his woman to come up with and to hold their shared vision. In couples where the man has taken off his balls, or has given over the custody of his balls to his woman, it may be her ladyship who is holding the vision

Some examples of women in the public eye who have or have had great vision and are laser focused and driven to reach their goals are Queen Boadicea, Margaret Thatcher, Esther Rantzen, Paula Radcliffe, Oprah Winfrey and Nicola Horlick to name a few.

You probably would not be reading this book if you would not hold a vision for your own intimate relationship also. It may be that the reality of how your relationship has turned out to be is far removed from the vision you had when you first entered the relationship.

The vision for the family is something you need to hold jointly with your man. If a man has not got a vision to pursue he is like a boat bobbing on the waves, only directed by wind and currents. He will become indecisive, uncertain, frustrated and resentful. In due course this may even result in physical discomfort and ailments. He may indulge in habits such as smoking, drinking and over-eating to mask the root of his feelings of dissatisfaction and failure. If you have children, they may start to resent their father for his indecisiveness, his perceived weakness and inability to be their role model and hero. This enhances and ingrains the feelings of incompetence he already felt, making the situation worse. I hear of many instances where fathers are 'found out' by their teenage sons. They have not got a vision and their sons challenge them, ridicule them and ultimately walk all over them.

Here is an example of a woman who has great vision and a large amount of masculine energy in her career and is unable to switch to her natural feminine state when at home with her husband.

Mandy is a stunning looking 35 year old woman. She is slim, tall and toned and always wears a sharp looking skirt or trouser suit that is made of excellent materials and is beautifully cut to make the most of her exquisite figure. She tends to look tanned all year round, as she is often able to whisk away for a long weekend to the house in the Algarve that she and her husband Darren own. Mandy is a successful entrepreneur and owns her own consulting business. She has a degree in marketing and human resources and gets called into companies that have problems with their turnover. She has been the one, time and time again, to put remedies in place and make companies that were on the verge of going bankrupt sound again. She looks into whether employees are in the right position according to their strengths and weaknesses, whether the right amount of work would have been put to one individual or whether too much or too little work would be placed on one persons' plate. She looks into the equal division of tasks between the genders, hiring and firing of people, the balance within the teams and whether communication between the different departments within the company functions or fails. She looks into marketing campaigns and finds out if the turnover increases according to the amount of money invested or not. She conducts her studies thoroughly, is direct in her communication and is appreciated and admired for the results her solutions get. During her working day, Mandy has to tap into her masculine energy a lot. She needs to be driven, hold a vision and be focused on meeting deadlines. She must keep her eye on the outcome and constantly task other people in order to leverage a large workload. She must listen to the problems her clients convey without being distracted by what is going on around her. It is impossible for her to spend a lot of time in her feminine energy in her career. If she would do this, she would likely be softly spoken when she needs to be sharp and raise her voice in order to make a point. She would be relaxed and distracted when she needs to be energised and focused and punctual to get the work done. She would talk about many different subjects, jumping from one to the other with no seeming connection, instead of staying with one topic until the conversation about that topic is finished. In short, Mandy would not be hired if she were to be in her feminine energy at her work most of the time. Mandy loves her career, the power it gives her and the buzz she gets from achieving her and her clients' goals. When Mandy returns home at night, she finds it tough to relax and chill out with her husband Darren. Darren is a doctor with a busy practice in a suburb of the thriving market town in which they live. The couple do not have children, as they are both busy with their respective careers and have put the wish to have children on hold. There always seems to be another good excuse to be found for not starting yet, being that the loft conversion was too expensive to have a baby now, or being that the possibilities for childcare in the town will be better in a couple of years time, so that Mandy, who does not have any intention to give up her exciting career, can keep on working. Darren is a gentleman who holds his lady in high esteem. He admires her ambition and is proud of his wife's achievements. As Darren wants his wife to be happy, he is prepared to put his own vision and the vision that he holds for them as a couple and eventually as a family, on the back burner. Darren was originally attracted to Mandy's gregarious nature and her boundless energy. Mandy instantly fell in love with Darren's even and good looks, his sense of humour and his ability to make peace between two quarrelling parties, a talent she does not naturally possess. However, during the last few years,

Mandy has become annoyed with Darren's complacency and has felt that she has been the one to carry most of their financial responsibility. She has lost some of her spark and works late more and more. Darren, being the good natured man he is, has noticed an unease, but has not spoken about it to Mandy as he does not want to rock the boat. He is also scared of her roaring bad temper during the numerous arguments they have been having lately. Mandy repeatedly asks Darren what he wants in life but Darren seems unable to reply anything else but 'to be happy with you'. This does not satisfy Mandy at all, and she keeps on and on at him with the same question. Darren is confused and unable to move on. He started to withdraw in his hobby of sailing small boats, without his wife, in order to escape the continuous interrogations. He is able to relax as his dinghy bobs about on the local lake. As he has become depressed and frustrated by the situation, he has subscribed an anti-depressant for himself that he has been taking for a few months now. He eventually came to me for coaching because he felt that he would end up losing his wife and his sanity if he would not take action soon. We looked at the situation and found that he was living in no mans' land with regards to his masculine energy, did not hold a vision for the future and felt he was living a life without purpose. One of the worst things for a man is to live a life without a purpose. I tasked Darren with reviewing his lost visions, goals, dreams and ambitions. He remembered and rekindled some and started discussing them with Mandy. Many of these did not fit in with Mandy's own goals, but talking about them enabled Mandy to see that her man at least did have goals of his own which gave her the sense that she was dealing with a masculine man once more. In follow-up sessions, Darren was tasked with taking his wife on a date that he had to organise for them, instead of her organising it. He began to use more masculine language such as 'I want' instead of 'I feel' and entered sailing competitions versus aimlessly floating around on the lake. He moved on to take charge of initiating conversations about holidays, the couple's financial destiny and setting joint goals for the future. In response to Darren's behavioural changes, Mandy slowly started to behave more feminine at home and clearly was more at ease and relaxed as her man seemed to have control over their future as a couple. It took them a good ten months but as Darren was steadily reclaiming his balls and vision, this couple was finally getting back to be the happy couple they set out to be.

When our man waits for us, does not interrupt a conversation or lets others go first (which can be just gentlemanly gestures), we can mistake his behaviour for being unable to take charge.

You will find that strong women who have successful careers and are happy in their relationship with their men are the ones that can be more masculine in their energies when they are in the world of their work and hugely feminine when they are with their man.

My client Claire was very focused on her vision for the future. She was an architect and had been involved in the planning, building and decision making for quite a few prestigious building projects. She loved the thrill, the power and the visionary aspect of her career. She had been longing to return to her exciting occupation for some years now. She had been taking time off to raise two young children who were teenagers now. When she became pregnant with Maisy, she loved working right up to the birth of the baby. Maisy was an easy baby and slept a lot, so every once in a while, Claire was able to take on a small architectural assignment to keep her hand in and to ensure that she was up to date with the latest developments in the field. Her supportive husband Dan had set up her drawing board in the cellar, which overlooked the garden and was a lovely light and spacious room. When her son Adrian was born fifteen months after his sister, Claire had to put her career on hold. With Adrian a baby and Maisy a small toddler, there was plenty to keep her busy and her days were filled with childcare, such as changing nappies, reading stories, building brick towers, finger painting, long walks in the park and by the seaside and cooking for her family. Claire was adamant that her two young children ought to get the very best start in life. She grew most of the family's organic vegetables herself and prided herself in being able to make yoghurt, sugar-free ice cream and delicious, healthy treats. The children were healthy, happy and thriving under Claire's supervision and loving care. Claire and Dan had been taking joint decisions about Maisy and Adrian's schooling, hobbies and sports activities. Maisy had done very well in the eleven plus exam and was able to go to the grammar school in the next town. Adrian also turned out to be a bright little button. He was just about to start at the local comprehensive secondary school, where he would take extra science, maths and dance classes to keep his lively mind and agile body interested and occupied. When Claire initially consulted me, she was eager to rebuild her architectural business and to be efficient and focused in doing so. We put a plan together that enabled Claire to slowly ease back into her old career whilst making sure her two children were taken care of as well. Claire hired a personal assistant who could man the office when she was off on site with clients. She got on very well with this lady and was able to ask her to do a lot of the administrative work, the answering of the phone and making phone calls on her behalf. Claire had brochures printed and followed a few courses to be more up to date with her subject and was confident and excited to be back in business. We stopped the coaching relationship when her objectives were met and she was able to continue on her path on her own. A year later, Claire phoned. She had just found out that she was pregnant. She had told Dan, and was initially contemplating an abortion. She felt that the family was really complete, and that a baby would upset her career plans totally. She felt that she could not take time away from her business for another child. In fact, she could see that if she would have another baby, her business could collapse and she was loathe to let that happen. She told me that she was so pleased because Dan had recognised that his wife was in no state to make an informed decision, being phased by the pregnancy and the emotion of the circumstances. He took charge of the situation. He took the pressure off Claire by hiring a cleaning lady and Claire and Dan sat down one evening to work out a plan where her very helpful assistant could work as her office manager. She was able to recruit a cousin who would help out in the office as well. In her feminine energy, she was able to put her faith and trust in her husband and they decided that she could have a baby and a business at the same time. She took long baths, she went for massages and slowly was able to unwind. When we spoke on the phone, Claire was excited and looked forward to the birth of her baby. She was able, with the guidance and support of her husband, to step into the uncertainty of the feminine energy and just trust things would work out. Dan had stepped into his masculinity at the right time, had taken charge and held the family vision. He had changed his normal attire of joggers and a T-shirt for more rugged jeans and a shirt, revamped his business to become more viable and mapped out a future that ensured security for the family for the next decade. It all worked out beautifully. Their little daughter, Andrea is now four years old, is totally spoilt by her big brother and sister and has her Mum and an elderly, Grandmotherly lady looking after her and tending to her needs. Claire has a thriving and growing architectural bureau which is well known in the local area. She is a role model for other women of what is possible when you stay in your feminine energy and allow your man to stay in his masculine energy.

How are you going to let your man have his balls back as the family leader? It can seem tough to give over the family vision, especially if you have been the one in control for so long. You may have references and examples of where your man failed! Bear in mind that it is only with practice that he will get good at this. Letting him have his balls back in this area is important. He will not take charge in the bedroom if he is not allowed to take charge as the leader of the family.

# Chapter Six
# The single woman

How do you give a man back his balls when there is no man in your life?

Well, provided that you want a man in your life, it could be that 'he' is not there because you are wearing balls yourself. I know that is a rather revolutionary thought and may sound preposterous but I would like you to hear me out and have an open mind whilst reading this chapter. It could well be that 'wearing balls' in one or more areas of your life gives prospective applicants the message that you are not worth pursuing.

**Why?**

If you are wearing balls in your career area, you can give men the idea that you have balls at home too, so they will not pursue you. A masculine man will not want to be dominated by a woman in the home. You may attract men without balls, who find it convenient that you have some, so you can be the one to look after him as well. What these guys seek is a substitute for their mother.

If you are in a high powered job, where you have a lot of responsibility and are in a position of power, it may seem impossible, but you need to transform yourself before going on a date, at social engagements and outside the work environment. You can also look at adding some feminine touches at work. Many women wear the equivalent of the man's suit to work. You can add a lacy top underneath, or some jewellery to turn it into a more feminine outfit. You can let your hair grow, creating softness and femininity or you may choose to add jewellery and accessories that emphasise your feminity. You can reserve a corner in your office for a fluffy chair, a lamp with beads, some candles, a pretty throw and some pictures that add a personal and feminine touch to the place where you work and spend the majority of your waking time. Even when you are the equivalent of the 'Bobby on the beat', you can add some feminine touches to the stark and unimaginative uniform you wear every day. Remember that you can hide your sexy lingerie under there! My dear friend Alice is a member of the special services. She spends her work time chasing villains and ridding this world of unkind individuals and gangs who live from the drug trade, child prostitution and other unpleasantries. You can imagine that Alice needs to be a toughie in her work and that there is not a lot of opportunity to display feminine qualities in her career. Even though she is the best part of six foot and as fit as a butcher's dog, Alice never fails to amaze me with her total femininity. She wears pretty underwear, goes out of her way to buy lovely tops and skirts and whenever she is in the Far East, where her work often takes her, she will have beautiful dresses and gorgeous suits made. Alice admits that she does make extra effort lately as she used to dress and be just like one of the 'guys.'

Jenny was a lawyer in her early forties. Her parents had been proud of her, as she was the first female in the family to have gone to university and have gained a degree. She was held up as the example for her younger sister, brother and cousins. Jenny was a role model in other areas of life as well. She was a talented hockey player and at the age of sixteen played for England whilst still at secondary school. For practical reasons, she wore her hair short and tended to wear comfortable clothing. She usually wore a pair of trousers of the out-doors type, a short sleeved polo shirt and a pair of train-ers. To go to work she would wear a white blouse with a dark trouser or skirt suit. She had some comfortable court shoes in both black and navy blue that she would alternate wearing, matching the colour of her suit. Jenny was in her early forties and had just been asked to become a partner in her law firm.

She was delighted as she loved her job and enjoyed the company of the other two partners, two likeable and handsome brothers. They had taken Jenny under their wing when she graduated and were pleased with how she blossomed and was able to take on a huge amount of the workload. Jenny had proved that she could hold her own, and Jonathan and Andrew were fond of her as if she were their sister. Jenny had her own office, which was stark, light and sparsely furnished. She loved her career and was pleased that she was still able to play hockey in the ladies first team of the local club. She lived alone, in a first floor flat, which was conveniently located for her work and where she had been for fifteen years. She had friends who she had known since univer-sity. On days off she liked to socialise, go to the gym or play her weekly game of hockey. She had had a few relationships with men but nothing much to speak of. Jenny started to regard herself as an old spinster and was wondering if she would ever have a long and intimate relationship with the man of her dreams.

Jenny consulted me a few times and it became clear that she was so self sufficient and quite masculine in her energy that she almost scared men who were interested in her. She drove a nice car, owned a decent flat and seemed to have all her ducks in a row, which could have deterred interested parties. To start with we set her the task to go shopping, let her hair grow a little and add some fun, little trinkets to her stark looking office. Part of her homework was to have fresh flowers in her office and her house continuously. She also went out and bought some more feminine looking training clothes. As she had a lovely figure, I tasked Jenny with going shopping with a friend who had good and feminine taste. She went and bought some great looking tight jeans and high heeled boots that showed off her shapely legs. The next time I saw her, she wore those, with a low cut top and some dangly, sparkly ear rings. She looked transformed and fabulously feminine! She told me that it was a huge stretch and that the heels were uncomfortable at times, but she gradually got used to looking (and feeling!) more feminine. Over time, she would still wear combat trousers, but she watched out that they were a fun colour and always had some frilly detail or other to offset the masculine details. In due course, Jenny managed to find her own style that was feminine, comfortable and unusual. When walking through the courtrooms, she had started to notice that men looked at her and sure enough, she was simply stunning. She was well on her way to being the woman she was meant to be. During a seminar abroad, she finally met a great guy, Joe, who actually lived in a little village close to where she grew up. They have been together for the last six months and the last thing I heard were rumours that Jenny and Joe are getting married in summer. Jenny had happily discarded the balls that were not meant for her in the first place.

You may be a woman who oozes that 'independence signal,' from every pore of her skin. If you are in this category, any guy who comes along will back off, as there is nothing he can add to your life. Your life is already complete without the addition of a partner, so he concludes (incorrectly) that he is going to be redundant in your life very soon. You must let potential candidates know that, if they turn out to be Mr. Right, they will be number one on your 'to-do list.' If it seems that you have your whole life sorted without the need for a man, he will pass your door, concluding that you are not in need of a man. Even when he finds you attractive, he will go elsewhere, where he is able to add value to a woman's life. Remember, a guy is in a relationship to make a woman happy. If you are seemingly blissfully happy already, there is nothing he can add.

Sophie is a single woman. She is fiercely independent and in her early thirties. She has long, wavy, blond hair, a cheeky, open smile, a wicked sense of humour and drives a BMW open top sports car. She has a good career and is head of the chemical laboratory with an agricultural feed company. Sophie gets paid very well in her job. She was able to purchase her first house a year and a half ago, with just a very small mortgage and is looking to buy an investment buy to let property. Sophie has two younger brothers. Sophie's parents are farmers and live two hours driving away from her. Sophie visits her parents regularly. She is fond of spending time nattering with her Mum and loves the debates she always has with her Dad. Sophie is the eldest child, and has suspected her Dad of being disappointed by her gender. She has always gone out of her way to please him and make him proud. It came to light fairly early in their childhood, that Sophie was the one with the brains in the family. Their father had always wanted at least one of his sons to go to university. When Sophie turned out to be more brainy than her two brothers, their father put all his hopes on his daughter. He was so proud when Sophie won herself a place to read biochemistry at Bath University and he positively glowed at her graduation. Her whole life had been one continuous story of success and independence. The only area that Sophie was desperately unhappy with was the area of intimate relationships. Sophie had had quite a few relationships with men. She seemed to always attract the wrong type. She went for the bad boys, as they seemed more fun initially. Once when she thought she had found 'the one,' she found out after having lived together with Eric and even having been engaged to him, that although he seemed masculine, he was a compulsive liar and had a drink problem that turned him into a violent man at home. Another one of her sad relationship stories was when she was at university and sort of lived together with Graham. Graham was two years older and was supposed to graduate from his sports medicine studies. Somehow she had ended up writing most of his thesis and seemed to be writing all the synopsis of his biomechanics text books. Certainly, she was fascinated by the subject but was less enamoured by Grahams' lack of ability to take responsibility for his own future. Needless to say that Graham failed his exams and after a few months, the relationship petered out as well. Sophie came to me for coaching. She seemed to have such a fulfilled life and gave signals to the outside world, that she was perfectly ok on her own. Men tend to be put off by this; she had balls and did not need a man to bring some more to the party. Sophie was tasked with being more in her feminine energy. What this entailed was to start delegating jobs at work, such as heavy carrying, fetching and doing errands. She was to go out more with her girlfriends instead of working overtime. She was to rethink her identity of 'independent woman.' She was to go out and talk with both men and women and tell anyone when it came up in conversation that she was actively seeking an intimate relationship and that this was one thing that was missing in her life. Word started to get out. 'Sophie is looking for a relationship!', 'What, you mean Sophie, the head of the lab, who seems so independent?' 'Yes, that's the one!' 'My word, I never thought she needed a man, she does not give the impression that she does.' 'It may be worth my while asking her for a date!' Sure enough, one thing led to another. Sophie has been on a few dates with different men, ranging from the company accountant to her brother's long standing friend Ben and a family friend who never dared ask her out before. She showed some vulnerability by expressing her needs.

She has changed her language and her identity. Instead of being an 'independent woman who can take care of herself and does not need anyone', she has developed into a woman who is happy with her own company and open to welcome a man into her life.

You seem to be unavailable. This could be because you travel, are busy with work or other engagements such as your children, your social life, sports, or your ex! Men tend to shy away when a woman is still somehow attached to an ex-boyfriend or ex-husband; they do not think it is worth the hassle. Maybe you are so absorbed by the exciting stuff that is going on in your life, that any potential candidate will be deterred by those seemingly unconquerable obstacles.

Debbie is always on the go. She is the taster and buyer of wines for a supermarket chain. This means she travels the world and has to spend time in remote places around the globe wherever there are vineyards to be found. I bumped into her on my way back from Fiji, when my plane was rerouted via Auckland to England. Debbie had just been on a wine tasting trip in New Zealand. Even though I could see that she could be attractive with a little make-up, she looked tired and a bit haggard in a comfy but shapeless tracksuit. I was fascinated by her career; I never even knew such an exciting job existed! She told me the fairy tale story of her profession. She painted a picture of lovely vineyards off the beaten track, ramshackle, but romantic farmhouses in Spain, donkey rides in Turkey and boat trips down rivers in South America. She told me that there was only one drawback. She spent so much time abroad with possible suppliers, in hotels, in airports and in airplanes, that it had been impossible for her to have a long term relationship. She was constantly on the go, lived out of a suitcase most of the time and when home, would just crash out for a couple of days before boarding a plane again. She did not organise her life very well and never knew when was the next time she was going to be home. She had a bunch of friends that she liked to hang out with but most of them were friends from school who now had their own families and were settled into family life. The few single male friends she had were more like brothers. Every time she met a man she liked outside her social circle, he was instantly put off taking things further by Debbie's busy travel schedule. We worked out that she had to make sure there were times that she was available and plan her life more so that she knew when she was home a couple of months ahead. She also agreed that she mostly dressed in rather drab outfits when not working and we decided that this was not the best way to show herself to the world. She said she would buy a few nice but comfy outfits to travel in and just add a dash of make up whilst travelling. She emailed me recently to say that she had started to date Mike, a divorcee, who she met in the airline lounge on her way to one or other exotic destination.

You can be the strong woman. The career woman who has made it financially. It can be that a man will be stopped in his pursuits for fear of being the one who is provided for, or for having to compete with you for the highest income. The man with balls will not want to fit in with your long term vision, as he has his own. Again, it will be easy to find a guy without balls who will happily slot into your plans. Ask yourself if this is what you want.

## Why do single women need balls anyway?

It is possible that a woman has had balls from a very young age. She could have been the eldest child. Maybe she was in charge of her younger siblings or she was expected to be a boy and disappointed her father. In order to please him she strapped on some balls and acted from her masculine energy early on. It could have happened later in life. During her teenage years she might have been the one who took charge in class and was chosen to be the prefect, or the class spokesperson in disputes. She could have been told never to depend on a man by her Mum (as so many of us have been). Later on in life, during illness of a parent, it could have been that she was the one everyone started to lean on.

## How do you get rid of the balls?

You may want to have a little ceremony to give those balls - that were never yours in the first place - back to the Universe (as there is no particular man to whom they belong). Just so long as you vow to give them up as you no longer need them. Bless them out of your life. If you have decided that you do need balls at times, make sure you hang them by the front door when you step into your personal life. Margaret Thatcher would have left her handbag on the hall table, thus leaving the balls of the nation outside her private life with Dennis. She would have had a change of clothes, brushed the familiar waves out so her hair was soft and straight and would have curled up on the sofa beside Dennis in her fluffy pink dressing gown with a Linda McCarthy ready meal, to watch his favourite TV show. So, have a shower, or even better, a long, hot bath, don your prettiest gown and mules and glide through your house feeling truly feminine.

## How do I recognise a man with balls?

Before you go on your first date, there are a few things to know. Men with balls phone women, they do not leave their phone number for you to ring them. Men with balls take you out, they do not ask for you to take them out. When you are actually on the date, know that men with balls make sure their car is cleaned before the date; they do not go through the carwash as part of the date. They either get the cinema, theatre or whatever tickets before you get there, or on getting there. They do not drop you in front of the cinema to get the tickets whilst they are parking the car. Men with balls will take your coat, get you a drink & buy you a meal. Men with balls will book a table at a restaurant or go to a place they know will have space available. Men with balls ring you after the first date. Men with balls do their own shopping. Men with balls do not conjure up their own personal wicker basket from the boot of the car when pulling up at Tesco's. Men with balls take charge in emergencies. When you are in the car together and have a prang on the motorway, they will ring 999 (unless dead or unconscious), take the other person's details and deal with all the formalities. They do not ring their Mum, their ex, a mate or hand you the mobile to speak to the officer in charge. Men with balls check out your flat for burglars when you have heard a strange noise. They do not wait downstairs in their car whilst you go in to make sure all is well. Men with balls stay when your three year old son has woken up in the middle of the night frightened of crocodiles under his bed. They do not run to the GP for stress relieving drugs because they can't cope with the pressure. Men with balls deal with their own crises at work. They do not ask you to be their therapist.

**Where do I find a man with balls?**

Men with balls are to be found in all layers of society, different races and cultures. You come across men with balls in all different religions and social circles. Men with balls can have had no education, some education and a lot of education. There are men with balls to be stumbled upon in all types of careers. Men with balls can be bartenders, bell ringers, or bookbinders. They can be nurses, nautical engineers and neurologists. They may be postmen, professors and personal trainers. In short, you can find men with balls anywhere. It just takes your -now trained- eye to spot them. Have fun finding them!

114

## Chapter Seven
# How to raise a son with balls and a daughter without them

In this era of equality we have learned and are careful not to stereo-type children. We are mindful to be open to give both sexes equal chances from the moment that they are born. We have long moved away from expecting little Johnny to become a lawyer and little Suzie to become a nurse. We dress little girls in denim dungarees, little boys can wear shocking pink t-shirts. We may give both genders stuffed animals to cuddle, ducks on wheels to pull along, balls to kick and throw, push along carts, paddling pools, sand pits, swings, see-saws, slides, tri-cycles and other toys to stimulate their physical and sensory development.

Some of us enlightened parents do not bat an eyelid when giving our toddler son a doll for his birthday along with a bucket of play dough and a box of building bricks. We slip our daughter the occasional toy car to play with and reason that this is all to encourage the development of gender equality. By doing so we hope our daughter may grow up open to the possibilities and choices that are available to her in later life. She may end up studying law, medicine, biochemistry or marine biology, carving out a career for herself in whatever field she chooses and enjoys. We trust that our son will become a sensitively natured creature who is kind to critters and people and will develop some degree of a caring nature.

When the baby is born, both parents mostly naturally bond with their offspring. When your man is allowed to do things his own way and explore his way of fathering, he will settle in a way to interact with his young son or daughter. He will enjoy intimate times of bathing, dressing, feeding and playing with his little one. A masculine man will deal with these matters in different ways than a feminine woman would do! As a Mum you may prefer your little one to wear this particular babygro, have the baby's hair combed in that particular style and restrict the feeding of your little one to certain areas of the house. You may not want your baby to be spoon-fed from the jar of baby food, sitting on your husbands' knee whilst watching the second half of the Man U v Tottenham Hotspurs European Cup match! You may not want your toddler to crawl through the flowerbed in her best dress while 'helping' Daddy weeding the garden! Guess what? If you want your man to be involved in the care and upbringing of the children, you must let him do things his way. So what if little Becky is wearing her vest back to front? So what when baby Joshua is wearing his pyjamas to play in the garden? As long as Dad is the masculine, adult and intelligent man you chose as your partner, he will, like you, have the best interest of his children in mind. It is healthy for your children to realise that things get done differently when Daddy is in charge than when Mummy is managing the household. It will give you peace of mind to be able to recognise that your sons and daughters need to spend time with their father. Let them learn to be flexible regarding their mealtimes, bedtimes, playtimes and type of play. They will soon learn and find out that different types of fun can be had with both Mum and Dad. They will come to Mum with a picture book, to Dad for stories about dragons and heroes. They will seek out Dad for some rough play in the garden, building of dens, cars and igloos. They will find Mum to put teddy's lost eye back in, for organising friends round for a tea party or making the dress for the nativity play.

If you want to raise a boy to be masculine and a girl to be feminine there are certain dos and don'ts. Boys and girls need to be able to tap into both their masculine and feminine energies. The section below gives specific ideas to support boys more towards spending the majority of their time in masculine and girls more towards spending the majority of their time in feminine energy.

**How to raise a son with balls**

**From the age 0-5 years.**

When a little boy is born, he gets treated differently than a little baby girl.

If the sex of the baby has been determined prior to birth, Mum and Dad to be, will communicate differently with a female than a male 'bump.' If the sex of the unborn is unknown, the words parents use are more generic. You can help to develop both femininity and masculinity in either gender. Boys are more inclined to venture out into the world, to climb, run, play rough, kick, hit, bite and explore more. Their large motor skills tend to be more developed as they have used them more at an earlier age. Their fine motor skills tend to be less well developed than those in girls of a similar age. Boys are more driven and less easily distracted from the object of their desire. They like to find out how things work and want to know the 'why' of everything constantly. That is the way they learn. That does not mean that you have to answer this 'why' question all the time, sometimes it will indeed be asked just for the sake of asking. If you ask him the rhetorical question 'well, Jamie, why do you think that is?' your son will soon understand that it is not only a question and answer game but a matter of thinking for themselves. Let him be in charge. When taking your young son on a train journey, let him hold his own ticket, give him the money to pay for his own 'shopping' and encourage him to hold the door open for Mummy. When you take your little man swimming, let him carry his towel, let him explore and let him find his own boundaries. You are raising a small boy to become a man, preferably one who is ready to be in a relationship with the world at large and in due course, with his own woman.

**5-10 years.**

Your little son is growing up. At this age, most boys develop a taste for sport and physical activities. Less masculine boys may still be daunted by the amount of physical contact in some sports. Your nine year old may hide in the changing room when rugby is on the time table as he does not enjoy playing rough. On the other hand, he may love it and find it a useful way to channel his enormous abundance of energy. Some boys really need a valve to allow their energies to let rip, in order to be able to sit still in class, behave orderly and civilised at other times. Take him to the local soccer club; have him explore the games of rugby, cricket, tennis, and whatever else is on offer in his school or your local area. Sports are a good way of preparing him to get to know how society works later on in life. Rules, particularly in team sports, encourage community spirit and thinking beyond the individual. He will learn to channel his energy in ways that it creates results; goals for his team and medals for his club or school. The boy is becoming aware of the increasing strength and agility of his body. Support his strengths and develop his weaknesses. If he is good at kicking a ball, but not good at sharing, he may want to join a soccer team, so that he can excel at what he is already good at and be taught how to play together as a team. Let him be independent within reason. Teach him to solve problems, so that over time he learns to deal with his own challenges.

**10-16 years.**

You are now starting to deal with a boy who is rapidly becoming a man. He needs to know his boundaries continuously and during this period will start to push them.

He is physically maturing and can be confused by his growth. He may need another male to reassure him about hairs sprouting from different places and body parts expanding beyond recognition. During this time especially, his Dad or another adult male can play a useful and important role. Both parents will be constantly scrutinised, criticised and berated for behaviour that was previously applauded and appreciated. Because your son is now forming his own identity as an individual separate from his parents, he will naturally start to question what before seemed normal. This does not mean he has lost or forgotten the family ethics and values.

**How to raise a daughter without balls**

**0-5 years**

When you have the delight to hold your little girl for the first time, there is a difference to the first moments with your son.

You will be more inclined to talk to her using words such as sweet, precious, tender, darling, honey and little princess. When she grows up there is a tendency to protect her and to take heavy tasks from her. A feminine little girl will be more into role-play to imitate her Mummy and other females, dress up, borrow her Mums' dresses and hats and pretend to be a Princess. She can play shop, pretend to cook and she is more inclined to include others in her play than play on her own. Her play will be about interaction and communication. Although girls can be equally inquisitive, they are usually more easily distracted than boys of the same age.

## 5-10 years

Girls in this age group really start to explore their world through communication. They make friends, and want to spend an increasing amount of time with them. They stick up for one another, share activities and talk endlessly. Traditionally the activities they engage themselves in are sports such as netball, rounders, tennis, and hockey. Other activities include music, drama and dance. Girls can start to become very competitive at this age and there is a discrepancy to be found in academic prowess between the sexes with girls outperforming boys. Their fine motor skills are more advanced and their handwriting is neater than that of most boys of similar age.

## 10-16 years

Girls develop into fully grown women during this time. They start to menstruate and are able to conceive. They can look and act mature, something that can fool many. Guide your daughter to explore her femininity, by dressing, talking, walking and behaving in a feminine way. Go shopping together. This is an age, where she wants to hang out with her girlfriends more than with Mum. The only quality time you may get with her is during a good old shopping spree. She may need guidance from both parents to encourage her initially and later on to veto what she is wearing and to make sure she respects the house rules. When she starts dating, make sure she knows to let the boy make the first move.

Your daughter may be predominantly in her masculine energy a lot. How can you support her and guide her to her feminine energy? She may be the proverbial tomboy. She may prefer to play with cars, climb trees, run, kick balls, wear trousers, get muddy and want to become a racing car driver. Do not make her wrong for this and leave her to do all that she loves. She is enjoying the boundless energy that she has and the body that allows her to do all that she wants to do. Let her know that she can do all the above and still be feminine. Show her options. She can wear pink trousers, have lush, long hair and wear pretty beads and still play soccer or rugby. Make sure that you as a Mum are the example for your daughter, shop together, encourage her to make herself pretty, go for facials together and spend girl time together.

Your son can be mostly in his feminine energy. How to support him and guide him to his masculinity? He could be a boy who wants to dress up, wear make up and put on his Mum's high heels. It is great for him to be able to explore all he needs to do without feeling that he is doing something he should not be doing. Let him use your lipstick and be the queen and laugh just as heartily at him as when he is dressed as the pirate or pilot. Let him spend time with his Dad or another male family member or friend in order to get some masculine influence. Single Mums may want to enlist their brothers, father or friends to take that role. Encourage him to play a sport, where the coach will become the role model.

## QUIZ

For women who are mothers or will be one day:

**1. Your baby is just born.**

a) You tell everyone that you only want pink clothes if you have a baby daughter and only blue clothes if you have a baby son.

b) You tell everyone that you want bright colours for either sex.

c) You do not tell anyone anything; you just wait and see what comes up.

**2. Your toddler son has fallen down and cries.**

a) You tell him that boys do not cry, to wipe his knees with a tissue and to get on with it.

b) You overreact, burst into tears yourself and don't let him off your lap for the next twenty minutes.

c) You check the damage, wipe his knees and give him a cuddle after which he goes off to play on the swings again.

**3. Your toddler daughter has tripped and hurt herself, she is sobbing.**

a) You tell her that it isn't so bad and give her a tissue whilst you return to the conversation with the other Mums in the playground immediately.

b) You overreact, gather your daughter up in your arms and rush to the A & E in the local hospital where you are told that it is only a graze.

c) You check the damage, wipe her knees and give her a cuddle, after which she goes back to play with her friends instantly.

**4. Your eight year old son comes home and tells you that Johnny has kicked him during the soccer match when the ref was not looking.**

a) You ignore his comment and tell him what is for dinner.

b) You phone Johnny's Mum and tell her what a terrible bully her son is.

c) You discuss the matter briefly and you both decide that if Johnny does it again, your son will have a word with him.

**5. Your eight year old daughter comes home and tells you that Billy has pulled her hair in class.**

a) You ask her what she has done and tell her that she probably started first.

b) You tell her to thump Billy one the next day.

c) You discuss it briefly and decide that if it happens again, she ought to attract the teacher's attention.

6. **Your teenage son comes home and tells you he has been suspended from school for a few days.**

a) You tell him he has to sort it out with his teachers, it is not your problem and that you have problems of your own.

b) You phone the headmaster and plead with him to let your son back in.

c) You enlist your husband to talk this over and come up with a solution to prevent future recurrences.

7. **Your teenage daughter comes home and tells you she is chosen for the leading role in the school play.**

a) You tell her 'that is nice' and continue checking your emails.

b) You tell her 'that is nice' and to get some money out of the bank to buy an appropriate costume for herself.

c) You and she discuss it, delight in it for a while and plot together what she is to wear and subsequently go shopping together.

**8. Your son has gone off to university; he runs out of money and phones you.**

   a) You tell him to get a Saturday job.

   b) You send him instant cash.

   c) You refer him to his father.

**9. Your daughter has gone to university; she feels lonely and phones you.**

   a) You tell her you have no time and to ring back at a more convenient time for you.

   b) You tell her to pull herself together, remember her vision and get on with it.

   c) You spend some time talking to her on the phone and when you are sure she feels better, you set a time to phone again.

**Mostly A:** You are doing both your sons and daughters a disservice; you may be mostly in your own masculine energy.

You may be busy with other important areas of your life. You give your children the impression that they are not important.

You give them an example of uninterested masculine energy. Make your children more of a priority and act from your feminine side.

**Mostly B:** You are raising ball-less sons and daughters with balls. Rethink your approach. Be more feminine yourself in order to be the role model of femininity for your daughter and an example for your son of how feminine women act. They are both getting confused and need more clarity and direction as to their own respective masculinity and femininity.

**Mostly C:** You are doing a good job; you are on your way to raise sons with balls and ball-less daughters. You are also staying well in your own feminine energy. You give both of them a good example of what a woman in her own femininity looks like.

## QUIZ

For men who are fathers or may become a father at some stage in their lives:

1. **You have just had a baby boy or girl. What do you do?**

   a) You phone your best friend and talk about the miracle for hours.

   b) You phone your best friend, go to the pub and get drunk.

   c) You support your wife, give her some nice jewellery, a bouquet of roses, marvel over the birth, do what is needed for the newborn and get back to work.

**2. Your toddler son is eating dirt in the garden.**

a) You tell your wife.

b) You jump up and tell him he should not eat dirt and wipe his face.

c) You ignore him and know he will stop doing this when he finds out that dirt does not taste nice.

**3. Your three year old daughter exclaims 'please don't hit me again, Daddy,' after she throws a wobbly in the local baker shop.**

a) You blush and ignore the stares of the other customers.

b) You tell your daughter off for telling porky pies.

c) You laugh heartily and give her a little play pat and gather her up in your arm.

**4. Your ten year old son has stolen a comic magazine from the newsagent around the corner and has been caught red handed.**

a) You lament at your wife that he will become a criminal.

b) You start to lecture your son, but your wife takes over after two minutes and you walk away.

c) You sit your son down and have a man to man talk about character, morals and your vision for the future.

**5. Your ten year old daughter is in tears because her teacher has told her off.**

a) You talk about it for hours and commiserate with her.

b) You say, 'o, well such is life' and go on reading the paper.

c) You listen to her and patiently let her talk until she has finished.

**6. Your fifteen year old son has been picked up by the police for vandalising a bus stop.**

a) You rush to the police station and plead with the officer on duty to let your son go.

b) You ask your wife to call the police station and sort it out.

c) You go to the police station, sort things with the officer on duty and make sure they put the wind up your son so he will not repeat the offence.

**7. Your fourteen year old daughter has lied to you and has gone to a boozy party against your wishes.**

a) You wait up until she returns from the party and tell her how relieved you are to see her back.

b) You ask your wife to pick her up from the party.

c) You pick her up from the party and have words with her.

**8. Your son who is at university has pranged your car.**

a) You say nothing but sulk for a week.

b) You tell him he must pay for the damage himself, but change your mind after a week and pay the damage yourself.

c) You work out a payment plan together with him and you both stick to it.

**9. Your daughter who is at university has been mugged.**

a) You sob for days and do not know what to do with yourself.

b) You discuss with your wife what needs to happen and let her deal with it.

c) You and your wife drive down and make sure your daughter is alright and stay with her so she can talk about the experience.

**Mostly A:** You are mostly in your feminine energy yourself. You are not there for your children; neither do you have anything to do with their upbringing or their future. They will remember you as some vague figure in the background of their youth that may provide the finances but has neither been an example, role model nor support to them.

**Mostly B:** You toggle between feminine and masculine energy. Your children may disrespect you for your lack of vision and leadership within the family. You may find it hard to be firm with your teenage sons and daughters. Your children may take advantage of you.

**Mostly C:** You are firmly set in your masculine energy. Your children know where they stand with you. You are an example and role model for your sons and your daughters get a sound idea of what healthy masculine energy looks like.

You raise sons with balls and ball-less daughters.

Whether you are a parent or not, you will very likely encounter children of various ages at some time. Think about your approach toward them, how you treat them and what type of example you are to them.

By starting when raising our children, we can prevent them from growing up as we did, girls with balls and boys without them, turning into women with balls and ball-less men. Know that you are doing them a huge favour and prevent them from having a lot of pain, challenges and heartbreak in later relationships.

132

## Chapter Eight

# A Chapter For Men. Do You Have Balls?

You are a man reading this book. Do you know whether or not you have balls? Are you wondering whether you have them?

How do you know whether you have balls or not? You can do this little QUIZ to find out.

## QUIZ

**1. You are sitting in the pub with some friends. A pretty girl walks by. What do you do?**

a) You haven't even noticed her.

b) When your friends comment on her, you nod and move the conversation on to something else.

c) You have a good look and appreciate what you see without feeling the need to make a lewd comment.

**2. You and your partner are going to the movies. What happens?**

a) She has chosen the movie and bought the tickets and you happily come along for the ride.

b) You have chosen the movie together and she picks up the tickets whilst you buy the popcorn.

c) You have chosen a movie that you think she'll enjoy and in advance you have already bought the tickets and a box of her favorite chocolates which are not available at the cinema.

**3. You and your partner are driving along in a city that you are both unfamiliar with. What happens?**

a) You read the paper whilst she insists on navigating and driving.

b) You both pour over the map and have an argument and you get hopelessly lost.

c) Even though you are lost, you know how to read a map. You pull over, find out on the map where to go and drive straight there.

**4. You and your woman are having an argument. Which is the most likely scenario?**

a) You try to placate her whist she is in a rage. This doesn't work so you start to sulk.

b) You are both throwing daggers with words. First you each storm off in a huff, then you later talk.

c) You are upset with your woman. She starts to cry. You put your arms around her and you make up without having to back down from your position.

**5. What are you most likely to be overheard saying?**

a) I don't really know. Do you have any idea?

b) I think this, what do you think?

c) I'll handle it. It's sorted.

**6. You go on holiday with your wife. What do you pack?**

a) Whatever she tells me to.

b) We pack together and have lengthy discussions about each item.

c) Two changes of underwear, one clean shirt and a fishing rod.

**7. The children are having an argument. It looks as if one of them is going to get badly hurt. What do you do?**

a) You ask your wife to sort it out.

b) You distract the children.

c) You intervene and give each child a task to do to keep them occupied.

**8. You have to work late in the office. What do you do?**

a) You phone your wife and grovel for her permission to stay late.

b) You ask your secretary to phone your wife to tell her.

c) You phone your wife, explain the situation and tell her you love her.

9. **You want to make love to your woman. You are in bed, what do you do?**

a) Whine about her wearing a nightdress without making any advances.

b) You ask her politely if she's in the mood.

c) You give her a foot massage, then with an evil grin rip off her nightie and get down to it!

10. **Your idea of the future for your family is:**

a) No idea, she's in charge and I'm sure she'll let me know in due course.

b) We have discussed this together in depth, but there is scope for change.

c) We know exactly where we're going and she knows that I'll make sure we get there.

11. **Your mother has moved in with you. What happens?**

a) Mother gets all the attention she wants, which is more than my partner.

b) I make sure I divide my attention equally between my mother and my partner.

c) I have let my mother know that my partner is the number one woman in my life who gets most of my attention.

**MOSTLY A:** You are not wearing your balls. You do not live in your masculine energy most of the time. Very feminine women will not be attracted to you. You may attract women who want to mother you, or control you in some other way. You need to strap your balls back on if you want to change the situation that you are in. Watch the movie 'Bringing down the house,' in which Steve Martin plays a man who has lost his balls somewhere along the way. His wife has moved out to be with another man with balls and it takes Queen Latifah in the role of Charlene to get him back into his masculine energy. A fun comedy with a message. His wife does come back to him in the end.

**MOSTLY B:** You share custody of your balls with someone else. At times you live in your masculine energy and at times you are in your feminine energy. The women in your life will not see you as a very masculine man and you will probably attract a moderately feminine woman. If you want to change this you need to take heed of the advice in this chapter in order to display more masculine behaviour.

**MOSTLY C:** You are wearing your balls. You live in your masculine energy most of the time. You will mostly attract very feminine women. Men who are not masculine may be daunted by you. You need to be careful not to expect male behaviour from a woman and instead cherish the feminine in her. You may need to focus more on her feelings.

Now you know whether or not you have balls. If what you have found out from this QUIZ bothers you, you may want to change and become more masculine. Here are ten tips to get you started.

## TEN TIPS FOR GETTING BACK YOUR BALLS

**1. Take charge!** Be the driving force in your relationship. Make decisions even if they are not the 'right' decision. You only get good at decision making when you make lots of them. When you decide (!) to make decisions you will feel in charge of your life and feel less anger, stress and frustration as you have not given your power away. This gives relief to your woman as she may have felt that she needed to make all the decisions up to now. She may have been overwhelmed by this, which made her tired, crabby and disagreeable. It will give your relationship more balance as your woman is free to be less guarded. She will be more playful and happier with life in general. You feel happier in turn. If you don't take charge in your relationship, the woman in your life will and she will feel tired, irritable and not admire you at the best of times. She will be angry and resentful and feel contempt for you at the worst of times.

**2. Stop being a doormat!** Many men have been raised to be gentlemen. This does not mean that you need to let everybody walk all over you. Express your needs and stick to your point. If you upset somebody, they'll let you know and you can apologise. When you stop being a doormat you let your true identity shine out and feel great because you are unstoppable. You feel that you can achieve anything that you set your mind to. You will experience more energy and you will get to where you want to be more effortlessly. Your woman will sigh with relief and feel that she doesn't need to do all the arguing and defending for the two of you. She can now focus on what she needs to focus on which is her warm, nurturing side that makes her soft and loving.

**3. Talk like a man!** Use language that men use. If you don't know what words men use, see chapter three. Sometimes men think that in order to be masculine you need to swear a lot. This is not the case. Masculine language is precise, to the point and uses words that express going forward and taking charge. This will make you feel more certain, confident and able to deal with the world at large. When you talk like a man she will feel that you mean business! She will be swept off her feet when you combine it with the other tips in this section. When you fail to consistently talk like a man you will be seen as weak by both men and women no matter what your real thoughts are.

**4. Walk like a man!** Stand tall, chest up, shoulders back, head upright and develop a strong male handshake (without breaking anyone's fingers). Think Michael Jordan or Russell Crowe. Walk with a sense of purpose, even if you have no idea where you are going. Stand, sit and move with certainty. When you use masculine physiology your brain gets more oxygen as you stand more upright and your lungs open more. Your chest will open, and your shoulders will broaden. These are all masculine characteristics. Did you know that when you slouch and hunch your bottom ribs dig into your abdomen? What happens is that your breathing gets hindered, your stomach and belly stick out and you appear less tall than you really are. With a masculine posture, you will notice that you command more respect from both men and women and this will make you feel more important and visible. A woman will notice this shift and be delighted by your change. She will feel safe and protected in your presence. If you do not change, women will tend to see you as a 'safe' but uninspiring option. They will seek you out when they need someone to talk to as they would a woman friend.

**5. Dress like a man!** Wear simple, neat, unfussy clothes. Stay away from too much detail. Keep jewelry to a minimum. Keep scents to a minimum. Even though you may enjoy facials and other body grooming, make sure you do not discuss those with your woman or go for more treatments than she does. Other people will approach you in a different way, take you more seriously and see you as more important, responsible and capable than before. This will make you feel more significant and powerful than you have ever felt before. Your woman will no longer have to hide her expensive feminine beauty products in case you nick them. It will create a polarity between you that means that your relationship will soar to new and unexpected passionate heights. If you use grooming products to a great extent, hair gels, many facial products, scents, waxing, manicures and pedicures, eyebrow shaping etc, women may treat you as one of their girlfriends (another safe option but not a hot date).

**6. Seduce her!** Make her feel special. Surprise her with her favorite chocolates, perfume, magazines etc. She loves your physical power and can go wild when you use it. Look out for clues of pleasure or pain to gauge what you need to do. Be direct and control the situation without overpowering her. You will notice that you are actually in control rather than wondering whether or not she is in the mood. She will love this new attention and will reward you abundantly. Your relationship will move from being average and on the boring side, to being exciting and you will both look forward to your next intimate time together. If you do not seduce her there is no excitement and no passion. Lovemaking becomes boring and a chore rather than the magic it can and is meant to be.

**7. Have a mission!** Know where you are going in life, what you want to achieve and where you want to be. Share the mission with your woman and incorporate her in your vision. Go towards your target without wavering. Challenges will come your way, like dragons on a hero's quest and they are there to be slain by you. You will notice many new opportunities arising. Your woman will feel that she doesn't have to do everything. Feminine energy naturally meanders and flows rather than heads straight for a goal. You will find that she opens up to you and is grateful to and appreciative of you for taking this weight off her shoulders. She will seem more attractive to you as she is able to relax more, laugh more and be more creative. You will feel you have made her happy and therefore are living your mission. It is like an upwards spiral. If you don't have a mission you are like a boat without oars or a rudder, floating aimlessly in the vast ocean of life. A woman loves to know that she can trust a man to get her to a better place in life without her having to take the oars or rudder herself.

**8. Lead your family!** You are the head of your family and it's important that you know where you want to lead them. Be the spokesman for the family. A lot of men think that the family is purely the woman's jurisdiction. If you give this power away you reduce your masculine drive. You give your woman permission to be more feminine by being the leader of the family unit yourself. This means being involved in the upbringing of the children by showing them what is right and wrong and guiding them when they go astray. It means being present and involved with the family daily or on a regular basis and being interested in their well being. This will make you feel that you are the chief of the tribe rather than an occasional visitor. Even if you and your wife are separated it is possible to hold a common vision for your children. Make sure you are involved in major decisions that involve them. You need to know what occupies them, their concerns and needs. When you have control of the destiny of the family your woman will be able to direct her focus more inward and look after the nurturing of the tribe. Because you will each be clearer on your roles, your relationship will be more peaceful and what man doesn't want his peace? If you do not lead your family, you will feel lonely in the midst of those who are supposed to be closest to you.

**9. Cut the apron strings!** You are a grown man now. Your mother will always stay special in your life. If you want or have an intimate relationship with a woman, that woman needs to feel that she is the number one woman in your life. It is not fair to let your partner feel she is competing with your mother for that special place in your heart. You need to let your mother know that she will always be your mother and she is special and unique in that role. You also need to let her know that you are now in a special relationship and that this relationship takes priority over your relationships with anyone else. It will make your woman feel that you are committed to the relationship and that she does not have to compete for your affection, time, attention and approval. She can start loving your mother instead of having to compete with her. If you don't cut the apron strings you will have the constant battle between your woman and your mother on your hands and you will feel constantly that you are being made to choose.

**10. Commit!** This is about taking charge of your destiny, even if you haven't felt like committing to the woman in your life before. Not committing is a sign of weakness and is un-masculine behaviour. Decide whether this woman is right for you. If she is, commit. If not, finish the relationship. So many men are heard to say 'I don't want to hurt or upset her.' What do you think is more upsetting for a woman? To be in a relationship with a man who fakes his love for her, or to have the prospect of friendship with a man who can admit that she is just not his soul mate and he'd rather set her free? When you commit either way, you get out of this stalemate position. You will feel that all other areas of your life move forward when you commit. Evidence from my Feng Shui knowledge shows as soon as you 'unblock' one area, others follow suit. You may want to take that into consideration when you notice that other areas of your life, such as career, finance and health are not showing as much progress as you expect.

Here's a little story to illustrate what can happen when you don't have balls.

Bob was a handsome man in his mid-thirties. He loved wearing soft-feeling shirts that were patterned or flowered. When I saw him at a distance he ambled along the high street from shop to shop. On meeting he told me he was looking for a particular brand of hair gel and asked me did I know where to get it. He had already tried the chemist while he was there getting his Mum's prescription. We got chatting over a couple of lattes and he told me that he had been going out with this gorgeous woman Tina since we had last met. They had been together for the past nine months. He explained excitedly that he was totally in love with her. The first few weeks were complete bliss as he and Tina were totally immersed in one another. Bob confessed that he felt at a loss as he did not know how to progress any further with the love of his life. Tina was starting to demand where their relationship was going. She had wanted Bob to move in with her and gave him an ultimatum. Bob was beside himself with worry as he had no idea if a woman would fit into his life. He had no idea where he was going himself and the idea of being in any way responsible for another human being filled him with dread. He was even more worried about her recent loss of interest in sex, as any time he asked her she had some or other excuse to get out of it. 'I can't please everyone' he whined over his third latte. 'My Mum wants me to stay living at home, Tina wants me to move in with her and I don't even know if I can provide for myself in six months time. I really love her and I know she is the woman for me...'

Bob had lost his balls somewhere along the way.

If we gave Bob back his balls the scenario could look something like this:

Bob was an attractive man in his thirties. He wore a simple black cotton shirt which was obviously of good quality. When I saw him striding purposefully down the high street he stopped me and asked me how I was. As we hadn't seen each other for nine months he asked me to stop for a coffee. He told me about Tina who he had met six months ago. His mother had disapproved of Tina to start with until Bob made it clear that this was the number one woman in his life right now. I asked him about their plans and he told me they were about to buy a house together and move in over the next six months. He confided in me that he had already bought the engagement ring to surprise Tina on her birthday next week. At that moment our conversation ended because a gorgeous, radiant and feminine woman walked into the coffee shop. Bob jumped up and took the shopping bags from her and planted a passionate kiss on her lips. He proudly introduced us and pulled a chair up for his woman. They obviously had a lot to talk about and were immediately engrossed in each other so I wished them good bye and was secretly already shopping for a wedding hat.

Regardless of where you are in your energy, you can achieve your outcome using the above ten tips.

## Chapter Nine
# Trouble shooting

Congratulations, you have come this far. Your man is probably well on his way to re-grow his balls. Or you have at least made a lot of progress in detaching the balls that you were holding in custody.

This chapter is for when things do not work out, when you have found that you need more advice, tips or ideas to help you rescue your relationship. By now you know that it is well worth the effort.

Do this QUIZ to find out what the challenge is:

1. **You are a single woman, on your first date with a man and you find that:**

   a) You are taking charge in order to make sure that things happen the way you want them to.

   b) You are not used to not taking charge and feel out of control when you are out on your first date, although you feel relaxed and happy.

   c) You are not used to not taking charge and nothing happens because your date is not taking charge either.

**2.** **You are a single woman, and have been on several dates with a particular man you find that:**

a) At times you are ok not taking charge, but you whine and manipulate to get your way. You are scared to loose your identity.

b) You feel a bit awkward because you are not used to his taking charge.

c) You and the man you date are in limbo, nothing happens because neither of you takes charge.

**3.** **You are a woman and have been in a relationship with a man for some time. You find that when applying what you have learned in this book:**

a) You keep holding back in some areas of your relationship, mainly during sex, where you feel you need to stay in charge.

b) You are mostly ok and at times feel out of control.

c) Your man has moved into 'pseudo-masculine behaviour' and is violent, rude, abusive and obnoxious.

**4.** **You are a married woman with children. You find that when you apply the techniques mentioned in this book:**

a) You do not see him as one of the children but you still sound like his mother.

b) Your man has taken charge of things around the house and is not doing things the way you would have done them.

c) Your man constantly rings his Mum to ask for advice as you do not give him advice any longer.

5. **You are a woman who is separated from her husband. As you apply the rules in this book you find that:**

a) Your ex wants to control you and because of that you find it hard to give the man you are currently with his balls back.

b) Your ex finds it tough that you do not seem to want to do 'everything' together anymore.

c) Your ex still expects you to do his bookkeeping, his laundry and be his secretary.

6. **You are a single man. As you put in practice what you read in this book, you find that:**

a) You still let women take most of the initiative when out on a date.

b) You think you may scare women off as you think it seems that you want to control them. In retrospect, the women you have been dating all appear to like you taking charge.

c) You are frightened to ask a woman out who is very feminine.

**7. You are a married man and are applying what you have learned in this book. You find that:**

a) Your wife is scared to let go of the balls, still treats you as one of the children and still spends the majority of her time in masculine energy.

b) Your wife seems to enjoy your being in your masculine more but it is hard to get direct answers from her now. She also changes her mind more often than before.

c) You don't want all that responsibility thrown at you, thank you very much!

**Mostly A:** If you are a <u>woman</u>: You are not letting go of the balls completely, you are scared to give up the control and power that goes with having balls. You fear the weakness that comes with your vulnerability. Remember, the most vulnerable people have more true power than the ones who seem strongest (think of the numerous non-violent protests where those without arms were more powerful than those with weapons, such as Mahatma Ghandi and Martin Luther King). Vulnerability does not imply weakness.

**Mostly A:** If you are a <u>man</u>: Your woman is not letting you have your balls back yet. Own your masculinity by acting from your masculine energy (see chapter eight), in order for her to feel safe to let go completely. She needs enough evidence that you are entitled to have your balls back by having the masculine posture, by taking charge and by being the one who is in control of his own future through his words and deeds. Keep going.

**Mostly B:** If you are a <u>woman</u>: You are letting him have his balls back and are well on your way to a fulfilling relationship. Stick with it and be patient and persistent. When you persist you will have a fulfilling, passionate relationship and you will have more energy. You will feel younger, look younger and be more carefree than before. You will have more time, more fun and feel happier and more fulfilled.

**Mostly B:** If you are a <u>man</u>: You are well on your way to re-grow your balls or already the proud owner of a pair of brand, spanking new ones! Stick with it. Explore and experiment and have some fun with it. Your relationship can be one of the most fulfilling areas of your life and when you are fulfilled in this area, all other areas will be affected in a positive manner.

**Mostly C:** If you are a <u>woman</u>: You are letting him have his balls back and he does not want them back! If your man does not know how to tap into his masculine energy, let him read chapter eight of this book. Maybe he does not operate a lot from his masculine energy. Make sure you stick to your plan to stay in your feminine energy. It may just be too early to expect any results.

**Mostly C:** If you are a <u>man</u>: You have not reclaimed your balls yet, you are either comfortable in letting your woman have the responsibility for everything or you are not sure how to manifest true masculine energy. This is detrimental to your relationship and can have a negative effect on your health and your wellbeing. Read chapter eight and apply.

**How to rescue a desperate situation:**

**Scenario 1:** You are doing all you can to give him back his balls and it seems that he does not want his balls back. By now you have stopped treating him like one of the children. You are more in your feminine energy and you have adopted different language. Things seemed to go well until now. You have lost all control and do not know what the future brings. Your man is picking up his masculinity alright and takes charge of the family vision, your finances and he takes initiative. He has got drive, a vision for the future and is single minded on his way to his goals.

**Question:** How do I cope with the constant feeling of being uncertain of what the future is like? At least when I was in charge, I knew what lay ahead. I do not know where this is going and I feel unsure of my man's ability to get us where we want to be!

**Answer:** In the beginning it is hugely scary not to know where you are going! It feels like being on a theme park ride with a blindfold over your eyes. In the beginning your man is not good at wearing balls. He gets off balance with the newly added weight. He makes mistakes. Remember, that you only get good at something with a lot of training. This is the same with owning balls. Stick with the training. Stick with staying in your feminine energy. Opposites attract like the opposite poles on the magnet. Yang needs Yin, the sun needs the moon. When you stay in your feminine energy, he will eventually have to move into his masculine energy. Have patience, faith and confidence in both of you.

**Scenario 2:** You are getting into your feminine energy, and doing all that has been suggested. You have changed your language, you are wearing feminine clothes and you have stopped taking charge. It feels great not to have to do everything anymore. But, he is not doing his bit! He does not seem to want his balls back and is not taking responsibility. The mortgage does not get paid, bills are overdue, the summer holiday is not booked yet and you start to panic.

**Question:** What do I do now, that my world is totally falling apart?

**Answer:** Have you talked about this with him? If you just do your part without having communicated with him, it will take him a long time to find out. Your house will be run down, your children delinquent and your car dilapidated. You must communicate with him to start with. At times he will need persuading, cajoling and nudging in your new feminine ways. Leave him a little love note in his briefcase, send him a sweet, reminding email, bake him his favourite cake (still works).

**Scenario 3:** You are doing everything the right way, you are making strides in the right direction. You are becoming more feminine every day and your man is getting more and more masculine. Things are good in your relationship and you haven't really anything to complain about. The main problem is that everything has become so 'samey,' your clothes, your language and your family life. Even your sex life is getting so boring because he is in charge and can't think of anything different to excite you both. It feels better than before but there is no zest, no zing in your relationship.

**Question:** What can I do to spice up my relationship whilst staying feminine? I am bored with the silly 'girlie' clothes, the silly hair things, the beads and the frilly knickers. I really need some excitement in my life. My man is so linear and laid back that he almost falls over backwards.

**Answer:** I hear you, girlfriend. The masculine man does not tend to have a huge amount of imagination and creativity. Maybe you are now experiencing the most yawn inspiring relationship that may be a sure cure for insomnia. When I told you about not taking initiative, I did not mean in all areas and not forever. There are plenty of areas where a man needs his woman's input and initiative. As you have discovered, now that he is in his masculine energy most of the time, he is so focussed and does not waver from his goals or destiny. That means that he does not give you the attention you so direly crave either.

Do not whine, complain or take charge and get in your masculine energy again. That will only drive him away, think of fun ways to entice him down from his cloud, out of his cave or up from his D.I.Y cellar. My friend Sandy, who I admire for her feminine and wicked little ways of teasing, will get her man's attention by bombarding him with nuts. When he is most deeply engrossed in his work, she will first throw one, then another one and have silent giggles when he looks up. You don't have to copy my friend Sandy. Just think of some fun ways in which you can bring some more fun and excitement to your relationship. Make sure to be attuned to when he is really engrossed in something or just killing time. Remember that you will make mistakes in the beginning. Take it lightly and have fun with it!

**Scenario 4:** You have handed the balls back and are now mostly in your feminine energy. He has responded very well, has strapped his balls back on and is now taking charge, doing a wonderful job. You enjoy not having to do everything anymore and have more time on your hands. But you now miss being in the limelight, you feel that you are playing second fiddle. You feel less important than before and even though you are happy with your man having his balls back, there seems to be something missing.

**Question:** Is there anything I can do to feel more important? Being in my feminine most of the time makes me feel that I am somehow less important.

**Answer:** It will take some getting used to this new scenario. Your man has stepped up and is now the one to deal with challenges, to hold the family vision and to drive forward. Now you have more time and energy. What have you wanted to do for a long time? Have you wanted to take up a new hobby? You could start or pick up a career. There are plenty of other areas of life for you to feel needed, special and important. Or could you feel important and special simply because your man is now taking charge and you feel much more relaxed?

**Scenario 5:** Your man has his balls back and you are mostly in your feminine energy. Things are good, but different. In the old times you knew there was love between you and even though sex was always the same and you were not honest about what made you feel good and what did not, you knew there was a connection between you. You are exploring new ways and are so open and honest with one another, that it sometimes feels that he is someone else and you are a stranger to yourself.

**Question:** How can I feel the love that I know we have for one another on an ongoing basis? Now that he has his balls back, he seems less connected and loving.

**Answer:** As he gets more in his masculine energy, he will be more focussed on his vision and his goals and he will get less distracted by you. That may seem a contradiction, but what it really means is that because he loves you, he needs to be focussed on where he wants to go. His total dedication and drive is what he needs. When your man is focussed, he will not jump up every five minutes to take you in his arms to tell you he loves you. Use my friend Sandy's nut throwing trick or some other playful method to attract his attention. The best common ground to totally connect with him on the deepest level is during love making. He will feel the deepest love for you in those moments. Light candles and have romantic music playing in the background. Sample a sensuous dish together. Use some humour and lots of foreplay to get you in the mood. You make your man happiest when he is able to give you pleasure.

**Scenario 6:** You are doing all the right things, you are in your feminine and he is in his masculine energy. You find that you are standing still in your development; it seems that you are not moving forward. He is doing all the work, the finances, dealing with builders and head masters.

**Question:** What can I do to feel that I am developing, that I am growing and learning myself?

**Answer:** You now have time to do some growing yourself! Take the opportunity to learn a new skill, read books, or do a course, find ways to grow outside your relationship. Have you always wanted to learn a new language? What about picking up Japanese again, a language that you started to learn as a teenager?

Attend seminars? Explore all the avenues open to you and enjoy growing and learning.

**Scenario 7:** You have done your best to apply all you have learned. You bought the clothes, you have changed your language and you have given over the finances, the maintenance of the cars and the house. You have reminded him, sweet talked him, cajoled him until the cows came home and went out again and you are convinced that this is not working. He doesn't do his part and you are going back to the old ways. At least your life was working. Now you feel like a little dinghy on the Pacific Ocean.

**Question:** How do I know it is ever going to work? Are there any couples this never works for?

**Answer:** It sounds that you are looking for evidence. How would you know this is working? Are you looking for too big a result too soon? Sometimes we do not see the little shifts that happen. When a plane takes off, a tiny shift in its course of one degree will make a huge difference to where it ends up. You may not see any results yet, as you have only just started this process. I can guarantee you, that if you make just a few of the changes that I have suggested, you will, over time, see a change. Carry a little notebook around with you and write down every little change you see for the better. We are so trained to see what is NOT working that we do not see what IS working. It may be that you are still using a lot of your masculine energy. You get impatient, irritated and angry when things do not work out. These are masculine traits. Give yourself and your man a good six months to work through this. You may even need a year or more. I told you it took me the best part of a decade. This book will ensure it will take you less. And it is worth it.

**Scenario 8:** You have now moved into your feminine energy and your man is well on his way to move into his masculine energy. You feel that you used to bring much more to the relationship. You were always busy with thinking of new things for your home, things to do together, things to give to him and do for him.

**Question:** How can I make sure that I still give and bring as much to our relationship as before?

**Answer:** You can still give a lot. The fact that you are now a happier person, gives your man happiness. The fact that you are less tired and exhausted means that you give more of your humour, your love and your presence. And you have given him a huge gift; you have given him back his balls...

# Epilogue

I have thoroughly enjoyed writing this book. Because I know that it can play a part in rescuing so far desperate relationships. If only one person has been helped by this book, I will have accomplished my mission. Please let me know how this book has impacted you on **www.brigittesumner.com**

I have to thank a lot of people who have been a tremendous support to get this book out. My Msix mastermind group, Connie, Jane, Doris, Gerry and Alexander. My friends Alli and Dennis, Yvonne and Bryan, Louise and Reicke, Annamaria and Ray, Don, Ron and Clive for their great feedback. Matthew, Lionel's fourteen year old friend, who relentlessly kept asking me about the book every time he saw me, which certainly made me get on with it. All the couples that have appeared as examples and stories in this book, you know who you are, even though I have changed your names. My two sons, Jeremy and Lionel. May you remember to honour the women in your lives and have beautifully fulfilling relationships yourselves. My parents, Threes and Siong, who are long dead, but because they involved me in their perpetual arguments, I became wise and knowledgeable in the area of relationships from a young age. I forever wondered what happened to the lovebirds that I could remember from early childhood. I now know. My brothers, Ed and Eric whose various relationships have provided me with much food for thought and material for this book. My friends Ariane, Fiona, Tina, Suhki, Vicki, Loren, Marcella, Chris, Nigel, Huib, Marion and Rheinhardt, Marijke, and Jette for believing in me. The readers of The Best Of You website and magazine. My amazing friends at the Anthony Robbins Companies for encouraging me and being a sounding board for ideas. Tony Robbins, Gordon Merfield, Grand Master Yap Cheng Hai and Sifu Yap Leong for inspiring me and giving me the tools to start and follow through on this journey.

My coach and friend Jane for her ongoing belief in me. My mentor Judymay, for her tough love and wisdom. My publisher My Voice Publishing for their smooth cooperation and seamless, professional and friendly advice.

And finally, my husband Rex who has gone without many things as I was out saving the world, who not only has his balls but also his loving wife back.

## Other books on relationships:

Anand, Margot - *The Art of Sexual Ecstasy* Harper Collins

Doyle, Laura - *The Surrendered Wife* Fireside

Doyle, Laura - *The Surrendered Single* Fireside

Gray, John - *Men are from Mars, Women are from Venus* Harper Collins

Katie, Byron & Molly Katz - *I need your Love, is that true?* Three Rivers Press

Pease, Allan and Barbara - *Why Men don't Listen and Women can't read Maps* Broadway

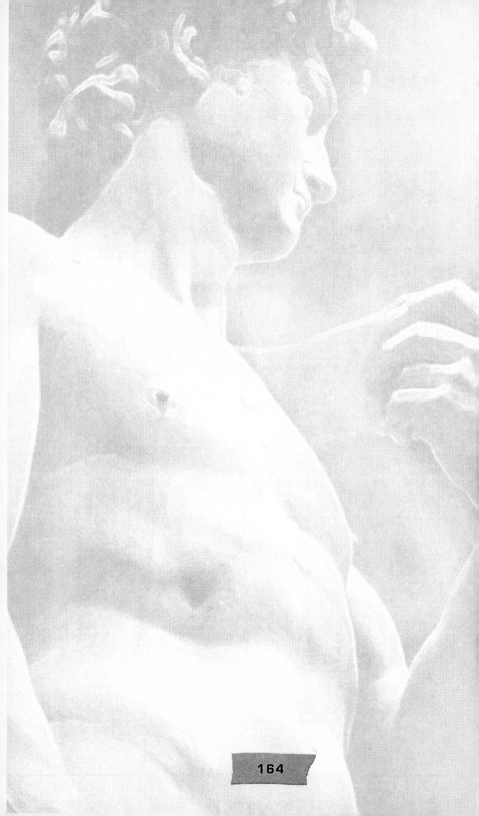

## Personal Development Books:

Breslin, Cathy and Judy May Murphy - *Your life only a Gazillion times better* HCI

Canfield, Jack and Mark Victor Hansen - *Chicken Soup for the Soul* HCI

Gladwell, Malcolm - *The Tipping Point* Back Bay Books

Gladwell, Malcolm - *Blink* Little, Brown and Company

Koch, Richard - *The 80/20 Principle* Currency

Robbins, Anthony - *Awaken the Giant Within* Free Press

Tolle, Eckhart - *The Power of Now* New World Library

Tracy, Brian - *Eat that Frog* Berrett Koehler Publishers

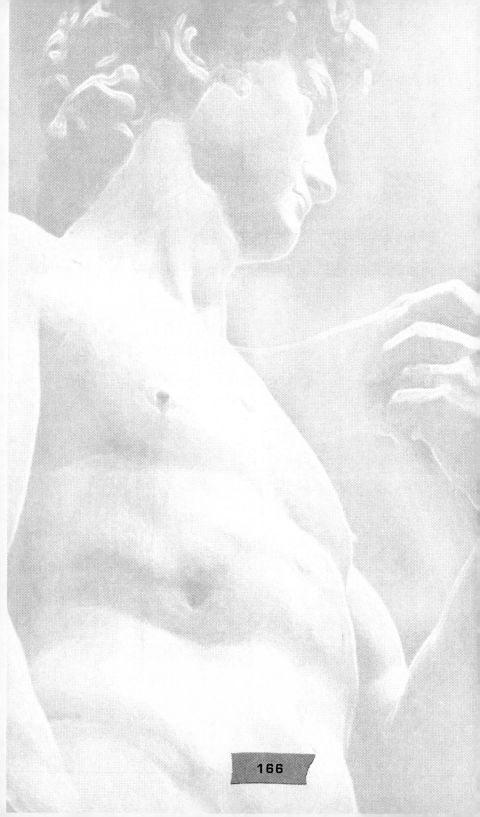

Brigitte Sumner is available for key note speaking.

For more information about books and products by Brigitte Sumner visit **www.brigittesumner.com**

Relationship and recharge retreats for singles and couples worldwide.